D0687714

Praise for *Create Your Future the Peter Drucker Way*

Create Your Future the Peter Drucker Way signals a new approach to the future for both individuals and organizations. Bruce Rosenstein reinforces why Drucker's ideas remain relevant for today and tomorrow."

—*Daniel H. Pink, author of* To Sell Is Human *and* Drive

In five succinct yet comprehensive chapters, Rosenstein skillfully draws on both his own wisdom and that of his mentor to deliver a plan for individuals and businesses in creating a future rich in personal and professional success. Leave your compass at home; all you need is Rosenstein's new book

—*Marshall Goldsmith, million-selling author of the* New York Times *bestsellers,* MOJO *and* What Got You Here Won't Get You There

Create Your Future the Peter Drucker Way presents Peter Drucker as a role model for designing and living your own future, beginning in the here and now. The book has expanded my understanding of Drucker's work and I'm confident it will do the same for you.

—*Chip Conley, founder and former CEO of Joie de Vivre Hospitality; author of* New York Times *bestseller* Emotional Equations

Bruce Rosenstein has opened the door to an important and often misunderstood area of Peter Drucker's work—why an understanding of the future is so critical for our development as leaders. It confirms my belief of a bright future ahead.

—*Frances Hesselbein, President and CEO, The Frances Hesselbein Leadership Institute*

In this concise and compelling book, Bruce Rosenstein provides a unique contribution: mining the nuggets of Peter Drucker's most important work about the future and presenting them in a brief, accessible format. Bruce is the ideal person to make Peter's work useful and valuable in this way. The quotes can be used as benchmarks and checklists to bring Peter's profound insights back into focus in a completely new way.

—*Bob Buford, Chairman Emeritus, Board of Advisors of The Drucker Institute; author of* Halftime: Moving from Success to Significance

Bruce Rosenstein has absolutely hit the mark with *Create Your Future the Peter Drucker Way*. Drucker was a genius of the first order and what he accomplished with his books, articles, and speeches changed the face of management forever. But Drucker told us what to do. He did not always explain how to do it. Rosenstein starts with Drucker's assertion that the best way to predict the future is to create it, and then shows us exactly how to do this. As the California Institute of Advanced Management's Latin motto translates as "Only you can create the future," you can bet Rosenstein's book is going to be pretty popular around here.

—William A. Cohen, President of the California Institute of Advanced Management, author of Drucker on Marketing, *and* The Practical Drucker, *and the first graduate of Drucker's Executive PhD Program at Claremont Graduate University*

Powerful, inspiring and full of practical wisdom. Bruce Rosenstein shows us how to apply Peter Drucker's timeless work to the essential task of creating our own futures. This book could not be more timely.

—Sally Helgesen, author of The Female Vision, The Web of Inclusion, The Female Advantage

Ever wonder what Peter Drucker would advise you about managing and leading your team in today's tumultuous times? Wonder no more. Bruce Rosenstein has written an engaging and practical look at how Dr. Drucker's principles can be applied to today's business challenges. Peter Drucker lives. Thank you, Bruce.

—John Baldoni, recognized global leadership thought leader, executive coach, and author of Lead with Purpose *and* The Leader's Pocket Guide

Bruce Rosenstein has done it again with *Create Your Future the Peter Drucker Way*! Fresh new insight, emerging from great analysis and synthesis, has become a well-earned Rosenstein trademark. Peter Drucker taught that the best way to predict the future was to create it. Bruce has moved his ideas forward in important ways, helping us to create a bright future by being more Drucker-like in the present moment.

—Jack Bergstrand, CEO, Brand Velocity, Inc.; member of the Board of Advisors, The Drucker Institute

Outstanding! *Create Your Future the Peter Drucker Way* is a brilliant book that translates Drucker's wisdom into advice you can easily put into practice in your organization and your own life. Developing a "future-oriented mindset" provides an anchor and a beacon amidst the turbulence of our times. Bruce Rosenstein's engaging and easy to read book is filled with actionable suggestions and a wealth of resources—a guidebook for a journey we all must take if we are to create the future we desire.

—Jesse Lyn Stoner, founder, Seapoint Center; co-author,
Full Steam Ahead! Unleash the Power of
Vision in Your Work and Your Life

Leadership of the future will be defined by not just what we do, but who we are. Bruce Rosenstein brings the best of Peter Drucker's thinking required to be our best selves. This book shows readers how to find problems, focus on opportunities and create solutions that are more than just good ... they are sustainable.

—Jason W. Womack, author of Your Best Just Got Better

Though Peter Drucker often said that it was impossible to predict the future, in fact many of his ideas about the "knowledge society" have come to pass. He also noted that it was impossible to manage change, therefore the only way to survive and thrive is to create change. For individuals this means continual self-improvement and openness to new ideas; for organizations it means constant innovation. Based on these principles, *Create Your Future the Peter Drucker Way* is a great guide to staying ahead of the game, allowing you to take the long view of your career, life and contribution.

—Tom Butler-Bowdon, author of 50 Self-Help Classics,
50 Psychology Classics *and* Think Long:
Why It's Never Too Late To Be Great

Bruce Rosenstein shows that cultivating the inner life is crucial for personal and organizational success in the future. He provides valuable insight from the work of Peter Drucker and others to show how our sense of hope for a better future can be deepened and strengthened.

—Bruna Martinuzzi, author of Presenting with Credibility: Practical
Tools and Techniques for Effective Presentations
and The Leader as a Mensch: Become the
Kind of Person Others Want to Follow

CREATE YOUR FUTURE THE PETER DRUCKER WAY

CREATE YOUR FUTURE
THE PETER
DRUCKER WAY

Developing and Applying a Forward-Focused Mindset

BRUCE ROSENSTEIN

New York   Chicago   San Francisco   Athens   London
Madrid   Mexico City   Milan   New Delhi
Singapore   Sydney   Toronto

1 2 3 4 5 6 7 8 9 0   DOC/DOC   1 0 9 8 7 6 5 4 3

ISBN   978-0-07-182080-6
MHID   0-07-182080-9

e-ISBN   978-0-07-182079-0
e-MHID   0-07-182079-5

Library of Congress Cataloging-in-Publication Data

Rosenstein, Bruce.
    Create your future the Peter Drucker way : developing and applying a forward-focused mindset / Bruce Rosenstein.
      pages cm
      ISBN 978-0-07-182080-6 (alk. paper) — ISBN 0-07-182080-9 (alk. paper)
    1. Management.   2. Organizational change.   3. Change (Psychology)
    4. Drucker, Peter F. (Peter Ferdinand), 1909-2005.   I. Title.
      HD31.R72335 2014
      658.4'09—dc23   2013026925

McGraw-Hill Education books are available at special quantity discounts to use as premiums and sales promotions or for use in corporate training programs. To contact a representative, please visit the Contact Us pages at www.mhprofessional.com.

To Deborah, as we continue to create our futures together.

CONTENTS

PREFACE

The future is important and can't be taken for granted. So why don't we approach it more systematically, inside and outside the workplace? It often seems amorphous and hazy, which means we don't treat it as seriously as we should, even if we sometimes think that we do. During the past five years, we have received a harsh, ongoing lesson on just how different the future can turn out from expectations. New college graduates unable to find jobs are taking up residence on their parents' couches. Retirees are struggling with significantly less income than they anticipated, due to unprecedented low interest rates and a sharp drop in real estate values. Once-mighty companies are shrinking or going out of business, contributing to a stubbornly high unemployment rate.

Peter Drucker, who was known as "the father of modern management," had a way of thinking and writing about, and acting on, the future that was integral to his personal and professional life. He developed a profound central insight, that the future must be created day by day, person by person, rather than be left to chance or fate. I contend that his future-focused mindset was a key factor that led him to the highest possible professional achievements, including being awarded in 2002 the Presidential Medal of Freedom, the nation's highest honor for a civilian.

Unlocking Drucker's Secrets

Create Your Future the Peter Drucker Way aims to unlock Drucker's secrets about the future, in part by determining the approach he himself took. The book distills and articulates lessons to help you discover the disruptive events and trends that are currently happening, or have happened, that will have the greatest impact on your life and work, and how to turn these disruptions to your own advantage by seizing on opportunities, even if they come disguised as problems.

In the pages ahead, I build on Drucker's extraordinary work and see how it extends to our place in the world now, how it relates to where we are going and how we are going to get there. This book will help provide a roadmap for you, the reader; no matter where you are on your career or personal journey. Getting to the future is daunting, but I believe Drucker provided us with a precious set of tools.

To learn about the future, Drucker read widely and learned a lot from friends, colleagues, and consulting partners. However, given that he died at age 95 in 2005, he did not directly make use of the powerful social media and related digital tools that have changed the ways we connect and interact with people, as well as how we find and use information. This book will help you to consider the place of today's online realm in creating your future.

The future is too important to be left to chance. In the past, companies outlived people. Now it's often the other way around. Jobs are less plentiful and less secure than they were only a decade ago. Many professions continue to undergo profound change. That's why I have examined Drucker's body of work through the lens of how it applies to the future. It required rereading and rethinking much of Drucker's output. It is not too much of an exaggeration to say that he was preoccupied with the future (or its cousin, tomorrow), and it was a focus of a considerable amount of his writing.

The Future-Oriented Mindset

Drucker taught and wrote over many years about developing and implementing a future-oriented mindset. In *Create Your Future the Peter Drucker Way,* I have attempted to tap into this mindset and organize it in a way not only to draw out his best lessons, but also to direct those lessons toward work you can apply now inside and outside the workplace. The book helps to answer the question, What do you need to do right now to help secure a better tomorrow for you and those close to you?

The identification and application of the core elements of this mindset are one of the organizing themes of this book. The book provides an approach, framework, and guide to make the most of the present to ensure a bright future, both personally and professionally. It helps you to embrace change, by focusing on possibilities, while not minimizing or ignoring problems or difficulties.

Understanding as well as applying Drucker's approach may help you to alleviate (or at least feel less threatened by) the inevitable doubt about the future and the anxiety-producing realization that it is unknown, uncertain, and unpredictable. Precisely because it is all three we need a strategy for dealing with the future, something we can practice on a daily basis. Why is our attention drawn so often to the future? It taps into the angst and anxiety that rests in so many of us about jobs, professions, organizations, and the economy. A smarter option is to make our own tomorrow, rather than leave it in the hands of others, or to fate.

A Future-Oriented Body of Work

I have searched through Drucker's writings to find those that are most future-oriented. I believe he was leaving clues for us, and puzzle parts to be put together later, as to how we can apply his writing on this topic in any setting. What he advocated works in good and bad economies, and for individuals, as well businesses and other organizations. In this spirit I have aggregated, curated, and synthesized a considerable amount of Drucker's work and have presented it in a concise format.

In addition, I have included some of the salient scholarship and writings about Drucker that have appeared since 2005. This is a growing body of work that has appeared in books and articles; on websites (especially from The Drucker Institute); and at events such as Drucker Day on the campus of the Peter F. Drucker and Masatoshi Ito Graduate School of Management at Claremont Graduate University, in Claremont, California, and the Drucker Global Forum, held annually in Vienna, the city of Drucker's birth.

How important is the future? It is where we are all headed. We can't do anything about yesterday or the past (except possibly to reinterpret it or learn from it). We can make the most of today, but tomorrow is something we can also affect and influence now. Leadership luminaries Jim Kouzes and Barry Posner have said that a defining ability for great leaders is to create a vision for the future and help their followers get there. In their 2010 book *The Truth about Leadership*, they advise that "you have to spend more time in the future."

One of Drucker's central, profound insights was that the future represents almost a way of being, a mindset and an approach that should be ever-present in our thoughts. It can be seen in many of his book titles, such as *The Future of Industrial Man* (1942), *America's Next Twenty Years* (1957), *Landmarks of Tomorrow* (1959), *Managing for the Future* (1992), *Management Challenges for the 21st Century* (1999), and *Managing in the Next Society* (2002). That represents only a sample of his writing on the future, but it is enough to give you a sense of the emphasis he placed on what was to come, and how to get there.

More than a Quarter Century of Drucker Study

For the past 27 years, I have studied Peter Drucker's work intensively. I wrote about him for *USA Today* for over a decade, and in 2001–2002 I wrote a column about his work for *Information Outlook,* the publication of the Special Libraries Association (SLA). In 2009 my book *Living in More Than One World: How Peter Drucker's Wisdom Can Inspire and Transform Your Life* was published. It focused on Drucker's work on the individual, including self-management. *Create Your Future the Peter Drucker Way* extends the work of that book, to help both individuals and organizations (business and otherwise) build their best futures.

Living in More Than One World used considerable material from interviews with Drucker (including from my personal interviews with him conducted both for the book and when I worked for *USA Today*). Although this new book includes some Drucker interview material, its focus has been broadened to include interviews I conducted with thought leaders whom I believe can help us to understand how to work toward a bright future, personally and organizationally. I have also drawn on the scholarship of a variety of writers whose messages are consistent with and related to the premise of the book.

In 2011 I became managing editor of *Leader to Leader*, the quarterly journal co-published by the Frances Hesselbein Leadership Institute and Jossey-Bass. Hesselbein, who wrote the foreword to my first book, was a longtime collaborator and confidante of Drucker's; indeed, the name of the institute, when it began in 1990, was the Peter F. Drucker Foundation for Nonprofit Management. I have tapped into her insights in this new book, as well as the ideas of some of the world's top leaders who have written articles for the journal.

Chapter Outlines

Chapter 1, "Create a Future-Focused Mindset," builds on Drucker's belief on the need to manage your present reality and take daily steps toward building a better tomorrow for you and others. We will look at the basic elements behind Drucker's core beliefs and views on the future, such as that the future must be created by individuals and organizations, for their own good and for their own survival. The first step is to develop a Drucker-like mentality about the future, to see the world, and where it is headed, through a future-oriented lens.

Chapter 2, "Determine the Future That Has Already Happened," builds on one of Drucker's most prescient insights: that parts of the future can be glimpsed by the effects of things that are, in a sense, history. It explores how to identify events that have already taken place that will affect you and your organization, identifying tools that will aid you on the journey to the future. We will also examine whether—taking into account Drucker's misgivings about predictions—today's futurists and forecasters have meaningful messages for individuals and organizations.

Chapter 3, "Become Your Own Successor," discusses ways to stay in demand and take control of your future by developing a strong body of work, diversifying your output and building a Drucker-like personal brand. When asked by the Brazilian business magazine *Administradores* who, if anyone, could be considered to be a successor to Drucker, I raised the possibility of 'Drucker as His Own Successor.' We now understand so much more about him and his ideas because of all that has been written about him in recent years. That makes those ideas all the more valuable, and thus makes him worthy of being his own successor. If we continually produce the ideas, products, and services attached to our name, we can create future demand that will help us become our own successors.

Chapter 4, "Shape the Future of Your Organization," shows how you and your organization (business or otherwise) can profit from such Drucker insights as "Innovating organizations spend neither time nor resources on defending yesterday" and "Planning is not an event." It also focuses on how to become organized for change as change agents/change leaders within organizations, in spite of the call of the status quo or, worse, the defending of yesterday's products, services, ideas, and values. Managing change means creating change. Many of the insights in the chapter, and in the entire book, are applicable elsewhere: in nonprofits, schools, governments, professional associations, and elsewhere.

Chapter 5, "Build Your Future beyond Your Current Workplace," helps you identify challenges and opportunities that may or may not be work related. It focuses on how the future will unfold in such areas as meaningful retirements, "encore careers," learning new skills, volunteering, and non-work activities that provide not only fun and diversion, but a sense of meaning and accomplishment. It also looks at the potential role spirituality and religion can play in your future. This is an area of Drucker-related studies that has become more pronounced in recent years, and it is a fruitful subject to explore as we all try to age gracefully and to continue to live more meaningful lives.

The conclusion, "Your Future Begins Today," recaps the major points of the book and emphasizes the need for an organized approach to your future inside and outside the workplace. Above all, it is a call to action, in the formidable spirit of Peter Drucker.

"A Selected Reader's Guide to Drucker's Writings on the Future" succinctly describes the books and sections of books that contain his most crucial writings on this topic.

Finally, there is a brief Resources section of websites that will help you to create your future, during and after your reading of the book.

How This Book Is Organized

Create Your Future the Peter Drucker Way intentionally has a simple organization: each chapter is arranged thematically, with periodic breakout boxes containing quotes by Drucker. Each chapter is composed of subtopics under broad chapter headings of how to work systematically toward a shining future, even with all its difficulties and uncertainties. Chapters end with a brief summary of the main points, as well as a checklist of things to do and to try based on the topics discussed.

By the time you finish reading, you'll have a strong sense of how Drucker approached the future in his own life and work and how you can apply his elements. I feel a sense of responsibility not only to Drucker's legacy, but to the many people who continue to read and learn from his work. I hope that you will return to this book often after you have finished it for the first time; because the future is ever-changing, the messages within these pages will ideally resonate for you as you continue to pursue life's challenges and adventures.

Acknowledgments

As was the case with *Living in More Than One World: How Peter Drucker's Wisdom Can Inspire and Transform Your Life*, the list of people to thank in writing this section is long yet incomplete. Some of the names are the same, but others are people who came into my life after that book was published.

Once again, the list begins with my wife, Deborah Goodman, and for the same reasons as in the first book: her love and support through what was not always an easy process, and her formidable talents as a professional editor. She was able to help me think more clearly about what I really wanted to say, and helped me find the best language for expressing it.

John Willig, my agent, continues to be a source of strength, support and wisdom about the publishing world. He gently but firmly guided me to make a serious start on the project, and then to see it through to completion. It's hard to imagine the writing/publishing journey without him.

John connected me with my editor, Knox Huston of McGraw-Hill. Knox has been a terrific champion of my work since well before this book was written. I'm honored that he wanted to add my book to the library of Drucker-related books his company has published in recent years. Thanks also to all of his colleagues at McGraw-Hill for the work they have been doing on my behalf, and what they will continue to do in the future.

Patti Danos has been a wonderful friend, advisor, and counselor. She, John, and Knox have been voices of sanity and reason about how the publishing world works.

Thanks also to Richard Rothschild, David Andrews, and their colleagues at Print Matters, for improving my work, and making this a more coherent book.

I am grateful to a number of people who read portions of and commented on early drafts of the manuscript, including my brother Jay Rosenstein (who, like my wife Deborah, is also a professional editor); Alan Inouye, Lee Igel, Bob Weltzer, Marijke Visser, and Maury Feinsilber.

As with my first book, I received wonderful help and encouragement from many people at The Drucker Institute and The Drucker School. At The Drucker Institute, I particularly thank Rick Wartzman, Zach First, and the archivist, Bridget Lawlor. Although the institute has admirably digitized much of the material in the archives, Bridget arranged for me to see some of the gems that are not available online during my visits to Claremont.

At The Drucker School and Claremont Graduate University I thank many people, including Joseph Maciariello, Bernie Jaworski, Jeremy Hunter, Hideki Yamawaki, Jean Lipman-Blumen, Leslie Negritto, Jenny Darroch, Richard R. Ellsworth, Kathleen Fariss, Nola Wanta, Rebeka Arnold, Scott Benton, Jackee McNitt Engles, Diana Luna, Bernadette Lambeth, Mary Jo Carzoo, Brandon Tuck, and Steven Kim. Thanks also to Deborah A. Freund, the President of Claremont Graduate University.

Peter Drucker died at 95, before my first book was published. I hope he would think that the interviews he provided to me helped to make both books worthy companions to his own writing. I remain in awe of the achievements he made in his career of more than 70 years.

I remain grateful to the members of the Drucker family I have gotten to know over the years: Doris Drucker, Cecily Drucker, Joan Winstein, Kathleen Spivack, and Nova Spivack.

My life has been enriched through Drucker-related studies and research by meeting, learning from, and in some cases working with the likes of Frances Hesselbein, Bob Buford, John Bachmann, Derek Bell, Shannon Barnes, and many others.

Thanks to Julian White and his colleagues at Web Video Vision for their great work on my website, blogs, and videos.

I'm grateful to the people you'll meet in these pages who were interviewed for the book: John Baldoni, Sally Helgesen, Jesse Lyn Stoner, William Reed, Tom Butler-Bowdon, Emi Makino, Joseph Lee, Daniel Noll and Audrey Scott, Jennifer Garvey Berger, Jason Womack, Bruna Martinuzzi, Jack Bergstrand, Arik Johnson, Craig Fleisher, and Chris Hote.

My visit to Japan in 2012 to speak at the Drucker Workshop Seventh Annual Conference expanded my horizons in many ways. It also expanded my knowledge of the reach of Drucker's work. Thanks to the people who helped me before, during, and afterward, including Chikao (Chuck) Ueno, Tomomasa Yagisawa, Yasushi Isaka, Joseph Lee, Jiro Atsuta, Katsu Fujita, William Reed, and the many other friends I made during that visit that I continue to stay in touch with.

My father Paul Rosenstein died at 95 in 2011, before I began working on this book. He was a great role model in life, and his spirit continues to shine. I thank my mother, Harriet Rosenstein, for a lifetime of love and support, and also for being such a wonderful role model.

In a perfect world, every single person who played even a relatively small role would be properly thanked in these pages. Because this isn't possible, I hope others will accept my thanks individually—in person and in writing—in the time that lies ahead.

CHAPTER 1

CREATE A FUTURE- FOCUSED MINDSET

1

People must take as much control of their own future as possible. Increasingly even long-lived institutions have become unstable, and many companies can't or won't provide the security that earlier generations of workers could count on. Gone are the days when you could take for granted corporate or even government benefits.

In their 2010 book *The Truth about Leadership,* top leadership authors Jim Kouzes and Barry Posner write, "The capacity to imagine and articulate exciting future possibilities is the defining competence of leaders. Leaders are custodians of the future. They are concerned about tomorrow's world and those who will inherit it."

Peter Drucker's writing on the future was sharp and perceptive. In helping you to best understand his approach to the subject, I have organized into a framework his ideas on the subject, beginning with what I believe are the 10 main elements, Drucker's core beliefs about the future. These elements, outlined below, can be applied by both individuals inside and outside the workplace, as well as by organizations, business or otherwise.

Most of the readers of this book will be what Drucker called "knowledge workers." You depend more on brains rather than brawn in your daily job. Your work centers on learning, conveying, applying, and developing knowledge, based on what you have learned throughout your life and what you will continue to learn. The portable and mobile nature of this knowledge meant, Drucker believed, that you own your own means of production. Knowledge workers are found in a variety of positions within business, academia, nonprofits, government, and related fields. They can be leaders and managers, scientists, doctors, lawyers, teachers, information technology workers, clergy, librarians, archivists, and many other professionals.

Peter Drucker 101

Peter Drucker (1909–2005) developed an approach and a mindset to the future that permeated his work as a writer, teacher, and consultant. His working life continued for more than 70 years. It encompassed writing more than 40 books, contributing regularly to such publications as the *Harvard Business Review, Forbes,* and the *Wall Street Journal*; consulting for companies, nonprofit organizations, and governments; and teaching at a school that eventually was named for him, the Peter F. Drucker and Masatoshi Ito Graduate School of Management, at Claremont Graduate University, in Claremont, California. He was awarded the Presidential Medal of Freedom, the nation's highest civilian honor, by President George W. Bush in 2002.

Drucker was born and raised in Vienna, went to college in Germany, then lived and worked for several years in London, before immigrating to the United States in 1937. He and his wife, Doris Drucker, were married for 68 years, with four children and six grandchildren.

Before moving to Claremont in 1971, he taught at (in reverse order) New York University, Bennington College, and Sarah Lawrence College.

While living in London, he began an intense, lifelong interest in Japanese art. He taught a course on the subject during the 1980s at Pomona College in Claremont. You can read the illuminating 18-page essay, "A View of Japan through Japanese Art," in the 1993 collection *The Ecological Vision: Reflections on the American Condition.* He and Doris developed an important collection, the Sanso Collection. I attended the opening of an exhibit, "Zen! Japanese Paintings from the Sanso Collection," at the Ruth Chandler Williamson Gallery at Scripps College on the Claremont campus during the beginning of the Drucker Centennial in 2009.

He had many other interests in life, including mountain hiking, music, and literature. He engaged in intense, three-year self-study projects until nearly the end of his life. And though most of his books were either about business or societal issues, he even wrote two novels, *The Last of All Possible Worlds* (1982) and *The Temptation to Do Good* (1984).

His influence remains strong, and his ideas continue to reverberate throughout social media all day, every day. A number of books about him have been published since his death. For the 100th anniversary of his birth, there was a major, yearlong commemoration, the Drucker Centennial, at the Drucker School and the Drucker Institute. It began in November 2009 and ended in 2010. I was privileged to participate in 2010, as part of a panel of authors who had written Drucker-themed books.

In 2009 the *Harvard Business Review* published an extensive, 19-page cover feature, "The Drucker Centennial: What Would Peter Do?" It included articles by luminaries such as Harvard Business school professor and best-selling author Rosabeth Moss Kanter and brief "What I Learned from Peter Drucker" essays by Frances Hesselbein, A.G. Lafley (the recently returned chairman and CEO of Procter & Gamble), and Zhang Ruimin (CEO of Haier Group, China), among others.

At the same time, *Leader to Leader* published an entire special issue, "Celebrating the Peter F. Drucker Centennial," with articles by Hesselbein; Rick Wartzman, executive director of the Drucker Institute; Jim Collins, author of *Good to Great*; leadership guru

Marshall Goldsmith, and others. And in spring 2009, the *Journal of the Academy of Marketing Science* also published an entire special issue, "A Tribute to Peter Drucker," which included Wartzman's interview of A. G. Lafley and an interview of Drucker by Drucker School professor Jenny Darroch, one of the editors of the issue.

Drucker's influence in Asia remains particularly strong, especially through the considerable efforts of organizations such as the Peter F. Drucker Academy (China), Peter F. Drucker Society of Korea, and the Drucker Workshop (Japan). I had the great privilege of being one of the main speakers at the workshop's seventh annual conference in Tokyo in May 2012.

The best-selling book in Japan in 2010, with more than two million copies sold, was a surprise hit: a novel based on Drucker's work, loosely translated as *What If a Female Manager of a High School Baseball Team Read Drucker's "Management,"* by Natsumi Iwasaki. In 2011 Iwasaki joined the board of advisors of the Drucker Institute.

10 Elements of the Future

Drucker's approach to the future allowed for changing times and different eras. Within his work, the future is always "on" and always running, similar to a computer's operating system. My study of Drucker's teaching and writing about the future has led me to distill and delineate a number of elements, outlined below and throughout the book, that are crucial to understanding how he approached the future. Although he wrote and taught about these areas, he did not group them together in the manner I have done for this book.

Whatever is happening in your personal or work situation can be matched against these elements. Not all of the elements will apply every time. But if you think of challenges that lie ahead in terms of these elements, I believe they will provide you with a guide to a brighter, stronger future. We will return to these themes throughout the book, as we consider them for both individuals and organizations.

Think in terms of transformations when considering the Drucker future-oriented mindset. We are all aiming to make something different (and ideally better) of ourselves and our organizations, all the time. It is somehow easier to deal with constant, unrelenting change, risk, and uncertainty if transformation is one of our primary goals. Considering how you can incorporate these elements into your own life and work should help make it easier to navigate the world and to determine, through all of life's changes, what is really important.

Here is a capsule look at the elements, which will be described in more detail in this chapter and will be referenced to throughout the book.

Mindset. The best way to approach the future is to keep it in mind as you go about your daily life and work.

Uncertainty. The future is essentially unknown/unknowable, uncertain, and unpredictable. You can't assume that it will be similar to today.

Creation. Despite and because of its unpredictability, the future must be built and created.

Inevitability. Accept that a certain amount of the future has, as Drucker put it, "already happened," because of the inevitable coming effects of events that have already taken place.

Present moment. The future unfolds based on and because of the thoughts, actions, choices, commitments, and decisions that you are making right now.

Change. People and organizations must accept this as normal and ongoing and should be organized for change, driven by change leaders/change agents.

Reflection. The observations you make about potential futures must include the implications for your personal life and work situation.

Remove/improve. The future is created by systematically stopping what is no longer useful, while continually improving what remains. This represents the combination of systematic abandonment and *kaizen*, which will be described further below.

Innovation/entrepreneurship. Innovations in services, products, and processes are major drivers of creating the future. Entrepreneurs create valuable new enterprises for the future gain of society.

Risk. Continual change means challenges from disruptive technologies and disruptive businesses, as well as nonstop turbulence. Risk is ever-present, but doing nothing is often not helpful, either.

The Mindset of the Future

Drucker maintained a mindset focused on the future in much of what he wrote. It can be a valuable guide as you strive each day to improve your life and the organization you work for. I believe it is important to consciously, intentionally, and deliberately think about future implications for everything you do, as Drucker did in his own life and work.

Besides the foundational element of the mindset, thinking about and applying the rest of the elements are how you can further put this mindset into operation. We all want to cultivate a sense of hope and optimism for a better and happier tomorrow, even and especially if life is going well now. It is too easy to become discouraged and sidetracked. Drucker believed in understanding exactly where you are now, as a way of getting to where you'd eventually like to be. Adaptability, flexibility, ingenuity, and resilience are goals to strive for, especially when so much is uncertain and nothing can be taken for granted.

We have to consider carefully how whatever we read, hear, see, and experience can affect the future, for ourselves as individuals and for our organizations, our families, and our professions.

Unfortunately, it is easy to be overwhelmed by what should be done now to have a better tomorrow. There are competing demands on our time and unreasonable expectations we often place on ourselves. Then there is the blessing—and curse—of social media. Blogs, Twitter feeds, online forums, news websites: they can be wonderful to learn from, offering all sorts of exciting and promising opinions, news articles, studies, surveys, and so on. Yet the sheer number of these sources of information (many of them undoubtedly excellent) can be not only overwhelming, but also anxiety producing. For one thing, there is no way you'll be able to read them all. And for the ones you do read, there can be the nagging sense that you are still somehow behind because you are not implementing recommendations.

"Knowledge workers are likely to outlive their employing organization."

—*Peter F. Drucker*, Management, *revised edition, 2008*

Drucker was fond of saying that he looked out the window to see what was visible but unseen by many others. To do this, you need to cultivate skills of observation, of knowing what to read and to whom to talk. This will be discussed in more detail in Chapter 2 and throughout the book.

Managing for Results (1964) was a particularly future-oriented book, with a chapter called "Making the Future Today." An edited version of this chapter also appears in the revised edition of *Management*, published posthumously in 2008. It contains one of the early uses of the phrase "the future that has already happened." Here, Drucker also writes of "making the future happen," speaking to the idea of taking as much control of your own destiny as necessary and feasible.

He notes that "even the mightiest company is in trouble" if it has not worked on the future, because tomorrow inevitably comes, and it is different from what we expect. The world changes, and if we have not changed for the better, the consequences could be disastrous. He advocates not guessing about the wants and needs of the future and makes a bold statement that gets to the heart of the concept of creating the future, contending that "it is possible to decide what idea one wants to make a reality in the future, and to build a different business on that idea."

That idea could be narrow and fairly specific, but it should be entrepreneurial and capable of producing new wealth. It means being ready to identify and capitalize on changes outside an organization: changes in the wider society, in specific knowledge, or in the economy. It means commitment to the future you are trying to make happen and faith that it can happen, all the while understanding the risks and uncertainties. There is also scope for seeing how a powerful idea can have implications far beyond your daily work and what your organization does. You can put your most important resources to work to create something new and different, something more important than what you originally envisioned.

The Uncertain Future

It's important to accept that no one can completely know what the future will bring. As an individual, you can try to affect it, which is where the idea of creation comes in. The world is so complex that it may be futile to make predictions, especially to make important decisions based on those predictions. There is a high degree of uncertainty. On this score, it is helpful to recall the words of a British blogger, Mark Vernon, writing about philosophy in 2009. He was calling on the ancient wisdom of Socrates, whom Drucker often referenced in his writings. The genius of Socrates, Vernon writes, "was to embrace ordinary human uncertainty and doubt, and fashion it into a flourishing way of life." Reaching beyond the unknown in this way can point to major breakthroughs in many endeavors. I love the idea of embracing change, uncertainty, and doubt, rather than running away from them. This is obviously easier said than done, but this can provide a more clear-eyed sense of what is possible in the future and what isn't.

"It is the very nature of knowledge that it changes fast and that today's certainties will be tomorrow's absurdities."

—*Peter F. Drucker,* Post-Capitalist Society, *1993*

In *Managing for Results,* Drucker lays down two preconditions about the future. The first is that it "cannot be known." The second is that "it will be different from what exists now and from what we expect." Those ideas may seem obvious, but perhaps only in retrospect. Too often people and companies operate on the opposite, or differing assumptions.

Certainly, the world of 1964 looks much different from today. People have different attitudes and changing values. Societal institutions have changed, and technology has advanced considerably, as has science and medicine. We are considerably more globalized, and the media landscape has altered.

We live in a world of uncertainty, and things are apt to get only more uncertain and nuanced. Although Drucker wrote about the futility of predictions, he himself was sometimes labeled a futurist and made, if not predictions, what he called "conclusions." The number of things we can confidently "count on" dwindles all the time. Every day brings new surprises and new challenges. It brings requirements to do things that we did not think we would have to do. In dealing with these challenges, we also should investigate whether today's futurists/forecasters have useful and important insights. This will be explored in more depth in Chapter 2.

Creating Your Future

At the most basic level, this principle involves developing, on an ongoing basis, what you want to accomplish and work toward and how you are going to get there. It also means not putting off decisions and actions so far into the future that they lose all meaning. Create knowing that life will be uncertain, that there will always be risks, and that change is the norm.

A major statement by Drucker about the future was made in 1999's *Management Challenges for the 21st Century,* his last book of completely new material. I believe that he wanted to influence how managers and others could approach not only the (at the time) coming new century, but the future in general. In those pre-9/11 years, the idea of a new century and how it would be different from all that came before was on the mind of many. In keeping with the creation theme, he writes that "a growth industry that can count on demand for its products or services growing faster than economy or population manages to create the future. It needs to take the lead in innovation and needs to be willing to take risks."

The unpredictability of the future was brought home only two years after the book's publication, with the September 11, 2001 terrorist attacks and the wrenching aftermath that continues to unfold.

The ideas on future approaches that Drucker advocated remain contemporary and useful. In consideration of recent popular books such as Peter Sims's *Little Bets,* about the power of incremental approaches, it is instructive to read Drucker's words that "there comes a point when the small steps of exploitation result in a major, fundamental change, that is, in something that is genuinely new and different."

In a tribute written about Drucker in 2005, John Baldoni, author of such excellent books as *Lead with Purpose: Giving Your Organization a Reason to Believe in Itself,* noted that one of Drucker's great themes was in essence how to make the world a better place. To me, that is a crucial aspect of creating the future. The world constantly needs betterment, with endless tasks associated with it. It also has ramifications for how we treat each other as human beings, especially in the world of work.

I've worked with Baldoni in my capacity as managing editor of *Leader to Leader,* and I asked him for his thoughts about Drucker in relation to the future. "Two things that influence me most about Peter Drucker's work," he said, "are his emphasis on history and his focus on employees as assets. History shapes our future, and knowledge of what came before is essential to shaping organizations of tomorrow. Regarding employees as contributors is a bedrock concept that too often employers overlook at their own peril. Focusing on ways to develop those leaders begins with treating each employee with dignity and respect."

I asked Baldoni what within his own work and approach, Drucker-related or otherwise, would help readers of this book develop the right mindset and approach to the future. "My work does not focus on the future per se," he told me, "but what I believe it does do is prepare leaders for the future by teaching them the elements of leading effectively today in order to create a legacy that serves the organization well. That means, I focus on helping leaders solve issues proactively, that is, focus on what they can do to make a positive difference as a means of developing individuals as resources and as future leaders."

"The most effective way to manage change successfully is to create it."

Peter F. Drucker, Managing in the Next Society, *2002*

The Inevitable Future

When the *Harvard Business Review* published its 75th anniversary issue in 1997, Drucker was one of five thought leaders—the others were Esther Dyson, Paul Saffo, Peter Senge, and Charles Handy—invited to write for a section called "Looking Ahead: Implications of the Present." Drucker's two-and-a-half-page essay was called "The Future That Has Already Happened." This was a phrase that he had used previously and would continue to use, because it was fundamental to how he approached creating the future.

Drucker begins his essay with his familiar theme of unpredictability: "In human affairs," he writes, "it is pointless to try to predict the future, let alone attempt to look ahead 75 years." He then goes into the idea of looking at what has already happened "that will have predictable effects in the next decade or two." As he often did, he pointed to the analysis of demographics as a fruitful source of these changes, specifically, collapsing birth rates and the aging populations of the developed world. And he maintained one of the major themes of the last couple of decades of his life, the need for better productivity of knowledge workers.

"What has already happened that will create the future?"

—Peter F. Drucker, Managing in a Time of Great Change, *1995*

Although Drucker said that the future could not be predicted, he did believe that we already had the tools to know what the future might look like. The starting point is what is happening now and has happened in the recent past. This could be from studying demographics, changes in society, advances in knowledge, and so on. What do these changes mean, and what are the likely effects of these changes? You can then decide if these observations present opportunities for you, your organization, and possibly your entire profession.

In some cases, it might mean stopping doing something. It is one thing to recognize the wisdom in an idea such as this, and it is another to actually incorporate it into your life and business. You also have to face the fact that with such widespread access to knowledge, many other people (including your competitors) have access to this same knowledge. The important thing then becomes, what are you going to do with this potentially valuable information? The theme of Chapter 2 of this book is how you can build these insights about potential futures into your daily work and life.

When you think of Drucker's concept of the future that has already happened, your task is how to determine it and recognize the relevant parts of it so you are not chasing the wrong future, or somebody else's future. For instance, having knowledge of a particular inevitability might require more funding, schooling, or technical expertise. If you really wanted to proceed, how long would it take you, and how much would it cost?

"Any attempt to base today's actions and commitments on predictions of future events is futile."

—*Peter F. Drucker,* Managing for Results, *1964*

This idea can be extended to related areas about what we know and what we don't know about important events. Although the future is unknown and has yet to happen, you should realize that you know a certain amount about the future in the form of commitments (financial and otherwise, such as contracts and money owed and earmarked), schedules, deadlines, regulatory filings, and more. It may be distasteful to think about it and consider, but there is also the case of your mortality. Death is in our future, and the realization should make us appreciate the present and enhance our plans for the future that involves living life to the fullest.

An important and somewhat lesser-known book on the future is 1969's *The Age of Discontinuity: Guidelines to Our Changing Society*. It is one of Drucker's most wide-ranging books, with thoughts on business, politics, society, and world affairs, and not just as separate subjects, but how they fit together. It anticipates both the near future at the time and the 30-plus years leading to the new millennium. These discontinuities are subtle and gradual changes in the ways various parts of society are perceived. They are undercurrents that not everyone has noticed. Drucker ends the preface to the original edition with this: "This book does not project trends; it examines discontinuities. It does not forecast tomorrow; it looks at today. It does not ask, 'What will tomorrow look like?' It asks instead, 'What do we have to tackle today to make tomorrow?'"

The four big discontinuities discussed in the book are (1) new technologies and new industries to support and exploit those technologies; (2) a world, global economy, rather than an international one (Drucker delightfully calls it "one global shopping center," in a nod to his friend Marshall McLuhan's idea of the "global village"); (3) the emergence of pluralistic institutions worldwide, coupled with dissatisfaction with modern government and large, established institutions such as churches and universities; and (4) knowledge as the most crucial resource in society, which he identified as the most important of the changes.

Princeton University economics professor and *New York Times* op/ed columnist Paul Krugman, who won the 2008 Nobel Prize in Economic Sciences, devoted a column in 2005 to how prescient (and underappreciated) *The Age of Discontinuity* was. He called it a "prophetic work that speaks directly to today's business headlines and economic anxieties." Krugman points out Drucker's thoughts about coming turbulence for once-mighty industries, which have played out with a vengeance in recent years. One of the reasons this is so relevant, Krugman writes, is that "corporations can't provide their workers with economic security if the companies' own future is highly insecure." Krugman's own words turned out to be quite prophetic.

The Future Embodied in the Present

It is tempting to think that, if the future has not arrived yet, that it can be ignored, at least for a little while. Drucker stressed, however, that what makes the future happen is what you do today, in the present moment. Your actions accumulate and have an effect on what tomorrow will look like. This requires considerable thought about what you want your future to look like, and then more thought on how you are going to get there, with the realization that in some sense the future never really arrives. The roll-up-your-sleeves aspect of this is captured well in his words from 1974, "The future requires decisions—now. It imposes risk—now. It requires action—now."

Drucker's quote reminds us that the future should be thought of as something concrete and real, rather than abstract and speculative. It is really a related dimension of time, as real as the (ephemeral) present and the (bygone) past. These three short, interrelated sentences force you to see the chain of events necessary for the future to unfold. Decisions, risks, and actions are all necessary by-products. We might add thought, study, consideration, debate, and dialogue. Although this was written in the context of an organization or business, this sequence also works for your life individually, at work and outside of it.

There is also a kind of purposeful poetry behind these words, compelling you to think about and act on the future in ways you might have not previously considered. These areas can be difficult for people, and for businesses. Risk is always tricky, and we often try to avoid it or make it go away. Decisions can be hard to make, and pro-crastination sets in. The same goes for action. Perhaps you think that action about the future can be avoided because there are actions that need to take place in the present, for the present.

"Decision making is a time machine that synchronizes into a single time—the present—a great number of divergent time spans."

—*Peter F. Drucker,* Management, *revised edition, 2008*

In 2001 Drucker wrote "The Next Society," a 19-page guest feature in *The Economist,* which comprised the final section of the 2002 book *Managing in the Next Society.* It is highly unusual for *The Economist* (where most articles run without bylines) to publish such long fea-tures by guest contributors, but such was the demand and interest in what Drucker had to say about where the world was heading. As he points out in the preface of *Managing in the Next Society,* everything in the book was written before September 11 2001, "and no attempt has been made to update the chapters."

The specifics of what Drucker writes about here are perhaps less important than his attempt to organize his thoughts on the future, in this case based on analysis of current trends and events. This exercise is something that you can benefit from emulating: regularly and sys-tematically examining business and society to look for the changes and disruptions that will have effects on your life and work. People and organizations that want to thrive will determine the best ways of organizing themselves to consider systematically and identify opportunities, especially those that come wrapped in problems, threats, and challenges. We will discuss this more completely in Chapter 2.

Where Tomorrow's Decisions Are Being Shaped Today is the subtitle of his 1986 book, *The Frontiers of Management.* The *Wall Street Journal* quote on the cover is "The first of the analytical futurists and the first of the management philosophers." In the preface, Drucker posits that seemingly ordinary people (not necessarily those we think of as leaders) are, in the course of doing their jobs, shaping the future by the decisions and actions they are making day by day. This is a profound insight, as many of us probably don't consider that we are making our future, for better or worse, by what we do each day. He makes the point that "change is opportunity" and that these changes give us the opportunity to improve ourselves, our organizations, and, as an extension, our communities and society.

In his book *Time and the Art of Living* (1982), author/philosopher Robert Grudin expresses a related thought to Drucker's ideas: "All important actions are open-ended to the future." This can be interpreted as meaning that the actions you take now can have multiple effects for your future. It includes effects that are unpredictable and that you don't know the ways they will play out in the future. In the open-ended sense, it could be that actions will set off a chain of events that are even more unpredictable and risky than if you had done nothing.

Making Friends with Change

Constant, unrelenting change is the natural order of things, according to Drucker. If this is the case, you not only have to get used to it, but have to learn to thrive on it. Developing the future-oriented mindset that change is necessary and healthy can lead to significant breakthroughs. In one of his typically no-nonsense pronouncements, he writes in "The Next Society" that "to survive and succeed, every organization will have to turn itself into a change agent. The most effective way to manage change successfully is to create it." A corollary might be that people within the organizations must turn themselves into change agents. Note that you are aiming not just for survival, but for enduring success. It helps if you think of yourself as a change agent, in your own life, organization, and profession. Think how radically many professions have changed in the past 20 years.

Two sentences in particular go to the heart of my thesis in *Create Your Future the Peter Drucker Way*: "The point of becoming a change agent is that it changes the mind-set of the entire organization. Instead of seeing change as a threat, its people will come to consider it an opportunity." Later he underscores the vigilance necessary for creating the future, combined with its inevitable uncertainties: "But what about future trends and events we are not even aware of yet? If there is one thing that can be forecast with confidence, it is that the future will turn out in unexpected ways."

"To survive and succeed, every organization will have to turn itself into a change agent."

—*Peter F. Drucker, Managing in the Next Society, 2002*

A chapter in *Management Challenges for the 21st Century*, "The Change Leader," is the major statement in the book on how to approach the future. Drucker begins with the stark assertion "One cannot *manage* change. One can only be ahead of it." (This is reminiscent of his pronouncement elsewhere that, despite the popularity of knowledge management, knowledge itself cannot be managed.) He points out that change is the norm, not something that should be put off or that should not happen at all. An organization (business or otherwise) must, in a conscious, deliberate way, take upon itself the task of leading change. Because the environment in which it is operating is characterized by "rapid structural change," its very survival is at stake unless a successful future can be created by the change leaders within the organization.

Who qualifies as a change leader? Identifying this quality is seen as a central challenge for the 21st century. Drucker describes a change leader as someone who "sees change as opportunity." The leader "looks for change, knows how to find the right changes and knows how to make them effective both outside the organization and inside it." This is certainly a challenge, because not everyone wants to look for change in the first place. It also suggests that a process is needed for identifying possible changes and for determining what actions to take.

It may be helpful to think of change in terms of transitions, which we will explore throughout the book. This is the subject of William Bridges' classic *Transitions: Making Sense of Life's Changes* (2004, 25th anniversary edition). Change is often unwelcome, threatening, and disorienting. Transitioning from the old to the new can be difficult yet vitally important. Bridges writes that transitions comprise an ending, a neutral, in-between zone, and a new beginning. However we accomplish our transitions, we need to apply language and methodologies that make sense for each of us, as well as for our organizations. Bridges observes that, whether a transition is personal or organizational, "[t]o become something else, you have to stop being what you are now; to start doing things a new way, you have to end the way you are doing them now; and to develop a new attitude or outlook, you have to let go of the old one you have now."

Emi Makino is a great example of someone who has managed multiple transitions in life, and she is now embarking on a new one. We became friends when she was an MBA student at the Drucker

School, in 2009. After receiving that degree, she then started on her Ph.D. in management at the school, which she received in spring 2013. She was born and raised in Japan and has studied and worked in the United States as a journalist. She was also a journalist and broadcaster in Japan, as well as an interpreter.

Emi has now embarked on yet another transition, moving with her husband and three children back to Japan, where she is an associate professor of management at Kyushu University in the city of Fukuoka-shi, Fukuoka. After she returned to Japan, I asked her to write a few paragraphs about her impressions of her transitions in recent years. This is her response:

Managing a career and a family with young children can be overwhelming. This is especially true in Japan, where family life so often takes a back seat to corporate life. Proactively investing in my self-development has been my way of resisting being controlled by the whims, wishes, and fancies of a corporation so that I could pursue a life with meaning. Yet even with the relative freedom and flexibility that comes with self-employment, balancing work and life was a struggle. I kept dropping ball after ball in this precarious juggling act, each time with deepening remorse and guilt.

One day I reached a conclusion. Work–life *balance* was neither attainable nor sustainable. I was going to strive for *integration* instead. Researchers have suggested that we live by metaphors. The shift in imagery from balance to integration has had a profound effect on my subsequent career choices. A work–life integration mindset generates new opportunities. What I had perceived as constraints on my career because of my parenting responsibilities (and vice versa) could be reframed as opportunities.

Shortly after having our third child, we moved from Tokyo to Claremont so that I could go back to school. We knew it would be highly unlikely that we could find childcare for her in Tokyo. A work–life integration approach enabled me to seek ways to combine our family goals with my career goals. We wanted to give our children the chance to study abroad at a young age, and I was looking to further my education. As a result, I am now on a new journey that is taking me to a destination I had dreamed of as a teenager: a career in education.

Reflect on and Observe Your Way to the Future

Navigating the future is hard work. Drucker believed that when executives studied trends, events, the news media, and other sources for clues to the future, they often stopped too soon. The important, often missing question was, what does this mean specifically for me/us? This could necessitate talking with others in your organization or other stakeholders about possible actions that could result from your study, observation, and research. This stage of reflection and discussion takes place before any decisions are made or actions taken.

"In turbulent times, managers cannot assume that tomorrow will be an extension of today."

—*Peter F. Drucker*, Managing in Turbulent Times, *1980*

Whether or not you think of yourself as a top executive, manager, or leader, you can take responsibility for converting change into opportunity. It must be done in a competent, purposeful way, realizing its potential impact on many people, including people you don't even know exist. It means taking responsibility for tomorrow and for making decisions based on solid thought. Drucker makes these ideas seem challenging yet doable. He makes them seem like a necessity, a responsibility we would be shirking if we don't take them seriously.

I asked Bruna Martinuzzi, the founder of Clarion Enterprises Ltd., in Canada, about her own experiences in applying Drucker's ideas on the future and what she believes is necessary to think about for navigating that future. She has considerable experience in a variety of fields: as a manager, leader, writer, speaker, consultant, and teacher. She says that as she gets older, she is thinking about the "importance of all of us who are of similar age to consider what legacy we want to leave for the future. Everyone should ask themselves how they want to be remembered by their immediate family, friends, colleagues, community, networks, and even the world. Are they leaving their own corner of the world a little better than they found it?" We will explore more of Drucker's thoughts on leaving a legacy in Chapter 5.

Her approach involves Drucker's cherished quality of continuous learning. I also found it intriguing, because it embodies a Zen-like capability that reflects Drucker's spirit and values: According to Bruna, "One of the most effective ways is to encourage people to approach things with a beginner's mind. Not an easy shift, but a crucial one. I apply this to my life, but also challenge my clients to make continuous learning a priority in their leadership development."

I was struck by Bruna's comments, because getting caught up in preconceived notions and the tendency to do things as we have done them before can hinder a future-focused mindset. If you take the time to reflect on your experiences, you can be more alert to surprises. This holds true for both surprise successes that can be built on for future gains and surprising bits of information that can lead to fruitful new endeavors. The concept of the beginner's mind is embodied in Zen and was brought to the United States in large part by Shunryu Suzuki (1904–1971), the founder of the San Francisco Zen Center and author of the classic book *Zen Mind, Beginner's Mind* (1970). It begins with this definition: "In the beginner's mind there are many possibilities, but in the expert's there are few."

Remove What Does Not Work and Improve What Does

Drucker wrote considerably about planned/systematic/organized abandonment. This terminology can sound somewhat harsh, yet it acquires a somewhat different flavor when thinking of it in terms of the future. If you were not already doing a particular activity (or making a particular product, or providing a particular service), would you start doing it now, based on your experience and results? If not, are you going to keep doing it? In this context, it is paired with continuous improvement, or as it has come to be known by the Japanese term *kaizen*. There is considerable material about this concept in books and online. In particular, there are two compact and highly useful books by Robert Maurer, who is on the faculty of the UCLA and University of Washington medical schools: *The Spirit of Kaizen* and *One Small Step Can Change Your Life.*

"Without systematic and purposeful abandonment, an organization will be overtaken by events."

—*Peter F. Drucker,* Peter Drucker on the Profession of Management, *1998*

Maurer points out that, despite the Japanese name, the process itself originated in the United States during World War II. In a basic sense, thinking of abandonment and *kaizen* together allow you to consider things for their current usefulness and potential for the future. Drucker recommended it for an organization's products, processes, and activities, including the supply chain. In an individual sense, it can be applied to activities you currently undertake. Which ones should be scaled back or cut back? Of the ones that remain, how can they be performed better and more strategically? Applying *kaizen* not only improves the quality of what you do—and high quality is now a minimum requirement rather than a luxury—it can also lead, as Drucker claimed, to further levels of innovation.

Innovating for the Future with an Entrepreneurial Attitude

Innovation and entrepreneurship are familiar concepts now, but that was not necessarily the case when Drucker wrote his book *Innovation and Entrepreneurship* in 1985. It is still cited as a classic in its genre, with good reason. These concepts are completely about the future. They are about change, either incremental change (as noted above) or more radical change. Innovators change how we look at the world, what we buy, and what we no longer buy. They change how we study and what we read. Entrepreneurs sense or create needs that consumers never knew they had. The best innovators and entrepreneurs make the future a different, better place from their creations, products, or services. They influence and change the mindset of their colleagues, employees, and customers. There has been a burst of innovation and entrepreneurship in China, Japan, South Korea, and Singapore, all Drucker strongholds.

Individuals and companies in forward-thinking countries recognize that education and hard work, plus networking with the right people, are key factors in creating their futures. How can you influence the world, your community, and different people by the organizations, new knowledge, products, and services you create? Jack Bergstrand, the founder of the Atlanta-based consulting firm Brand Velocity, Inc., and author of a heavily Drucker-influenced book, *Reinvent Your Enterprise through Better Knowledge Work*, told me that he believes "creating the future links well to Drucker's thinking on innovation, and he had a wonderful three-part recipe for it. First, stop doing what is not working. Second, build upon your strengths. Third, do something new. Importantly, stopping was the most important and difficult step. It is difficult because we don't like to abandon things. It is important because it frees up resources for creating the future." In 2012 Bergstrand joined the board of advisors of the Drucker Institute.

"Systematic innovation requires a willingness to look on change as an opportunity."

—*Peter F. Drucker,* Managing for the Future, *1993*

In "The Next Society," Drucker writes that "grafting innovation on to a traditional enterprise does not work." This can have multiple meanings, but I take it to mean that if you always do things in a traditional way and are set in your ways, it is hard to become an innovative, entrepreneurial company or organization. I would argue that this goes for individuals as well, inside and outside the workplace. If you do not have the capabilities to carry out innovation, the question becomes where will you find these capabilities? Will current employees be able to change their thinking and actions? Might some of this come from concepts Drucker often wrote about, such as pilot programs, alliances, partnerships, and so forth? Can you borrow people or ideas to become innovative?

Another terrific writer I've worked with at *Leader to Leader* is Sally Helgesen, author of such classic books as *The Web of Inclusion:*

A New Architecture for Building Great Organizations and *The Female Advantage: Women's Ways of Leadership.*

She told me of Drucker's longstanding influence on her work and that "Drucker grasped, very early, the salient and determining fact of postindustrial society: that the fundamental role of knowledge in creating value in the marketplace gives workers control of the primary means of production, which are lodged within their skulls and get into the elevator with them when they go home. This shifts the underlying dynamic that shaped industrial society, the control of means of production (primarily machines) by owners. The result has been empowerment of individuals with the capacity to use their knowledge to create value."

Each year, the Drucker Institute gives the Peter F. Drucker Award for Nonprofit Innovation, with financial assistance from the Coca-Cola Foundation. The first-place prize is worth $100,000. The institute says on its website that the award is "given each fall to a nonprofit organization that best demonstrates Drucker's definition of innovation: change that creates a new dimension of performance." The 2012 winner was the American Refugee Committee, a Minneapolis-based organization that worked with the global Somali diaspora community for its I AM A STAR program to improve the lives of people living in Somalia. (Slogan: Creating a Better Future for Somalia.)

Each week, the Frances Hesselbein Leadership Institute features a "Profile in Innovation" on its website, focusing on an innovative organization, company, or program. Reading the profiles is a great way to learn about new, up-and-coming organizations and social entrepreneurs. It also provides a window into what is possible through human ingenuity and how that relates to solving problems and extending opportunities in society.

In the *Transitions* book referenced above, William Bridges notes that our economy depends on innovation. "If the innovation ceased," he writes, "our economy as a whole—and, of course, most people's individual careers—would fall apart." Innovation is closely tied to the idea of "creative destruction" associated with Joseph Schumpeter, the Austrian-born, 20th-century economist whom Drucker often referenced.

Risk Will Always Be with Us

Drucker pointed out that, although making the future was highly risky, *not* trying to make the future was equally or more risky. The element of risk is something we have to accept and factor in to our daily lives and decisions.

The concept of risk and being prepared for an unknown future relates directly to the unpredictability of so-called black swan events, as explained by Nassim Nicholas Taleb, in *The Black Swan: The Impact of the Highly Improbable* and other books. Such events are thought of as extremely unlikely to happen, yet if they do, the impact can be devastating. And Harvard Business School professor Clayton Christensen, who topped the "Thinkers 50" list of top management gurus in 2011, has written in books such as *The Innovator's Dilemma* about the concept of disruptive technologies and events that have the potential to change completely the way entire industries conduct their business.

In a 1975 article for the *Wall Street Journal*, "The Delusion of Profits," Drucker noted the risk and uncertainty inherent in all economic activity, which he called "the commitment of existing resources to future expectations." He identified a number of potential areas for this risk/uncertainty: what and how your organization produces, what equipment you use, the markets within which you work, and larger changes outside your organization. All contained risk, and in the case of businesses, a minimum profit level should be determined to cover these future risks.

"To try to make the future is highly risky. It is less risky, however, than not to try to make it. A goodly proportion of those attempting ... will surely not succeed. But, predictably, no one else will."

—*Peter F. Drucker,* Management Challenges for
the 21st Century, *1999*

Working as best as you can in regard to risk, especially risk for long-range commitments, is one of the things that Drucker said defined what it means to be a manager. The key is to make those decisions as responsibly and rationally as possible, with the most intelligent use of information. Somehow you have to understand the relationship between risk and security. In the book *Managing for the Future,* he writes that "risk and security are not in opposition, but parallel." Although these ideas on risk are seen through an organizational lens, it is individual executives, working either alone or in tandem with others, that must make these decisions. Likewise, decisions you make about your own career and activities obviously involve risk as well.

Conclusion

Any journey to the future involves preparation. Maintaining a Drucker-like mindset is essential. The elements above represent your guide, based on Drucker's writings and teachings, for navigating tomorrow. The key points from some of his books that we have outlined give you a further understanding of how he arrived at these essential elements regarding thinking about and acting on the future.

Both individual knowledge workers and organizations are moving inevitably toward a future that is created one day, one action at a time. Remaining alert to potential implications of actions and events seemingly tangential to the future is a valuable skill that you will begin cultivating in Chapter 2,where we will take a deeper dive into how you can keep tabs on tomorrow, by determining the future that has already happened.

Chapter Review

In this chapter we have outlined elements underlying Peter Drucker's body of work on the future. These elements represent a forward-focused mindset to life inside and outside the workplace. In Drucker's life and work, the future was like a computer operating system, continually at work as he approached his writing, teaching, and consulting. We've seen that in order to thrive and improve our lives, he advocated embracing change, risk, and uncertainty. Review what you do currently to remove what is no longer productive or necessary, while improving what remains. Above all, the future must be created in a purposeful, meaningful way, by the actions people and organizations carry out each day.

Checklist

My goal is for this book to be as interactive as possible. At the end of each chapter, there is a brief checklist of items to keep in mind as you create your future. The first list is intentionally short, as your journey is just beginning.

✓ Start a notebook or computer file (ideally both) on Creating the Future.
✓ As you begin to read this book, note your current attitudes toward the future and what some of your goals are, both personally and professionally. You can then compare what you've written to what you'll write as you continue reading the book.

✓ List three to five role models of people (either those you know or public figures) who seem to be adept at navigating the future.

✓ List three to five organizations (business or otherwise) you believe have the same qualities.

✓ Think of times in your life when you have applied the Zen concept of the beginner's mind. Consider ways that approach can be applied to future tasks and challenges, as well as to those you are facing now.

DETERMINE THE FUTURE THAT HAS ALREADY HAPPENED

2

The future surrounds us. It's embodied in the work, ideas, and insights of countless people and organizations worldwide. It can contain the seeds of considerable wealth and knowledge. In this chapter, we will go deeper into the idea of finding the future based on available information from individuals, groups, and organizations. As outlined in Chapter 1, Peter Drucker believed that a major task in building the future is to determine "the future that has already happened." This is broadly speaking the anticipation of the effects of events or trends that have already taken place that will unfold over a period of time. But identifying these events and trends can be tricky. While he believed that clues could be determined from such sources as demographics, changes in the economy and society, and developments in knowledge, he did not go into specifics about exactly where to find this information and how to keep up with it.

To put this concept into operation, you will find outlined in this chapter various sources and suggestions for helping you to make the best determination of potential futures. This approach relies not on making predictions of particular events, but on how to best keep up with world events to determine the best potential future for you and your organization.

If determining the future that has already happened were easy, anyone could do it. We would have a world full of people who are ready for anything that happens and able to create strong, successful futures. But that is obviously not the case. If your goal is to create the future, you should develop some solid strategies for learning more about potential futures, even though the future is unpredictable. To determine how to create the future, you should develop a solid understanding of what beyond your immediate surroundings is shaping it, even in subtle ways. This takes some effort and requires thought and concentration. But the people who can effectively employ these resources stand to create the brightest futures.

I have widened the concept somewhat to include additional relevant information that you can read, hear, or find online. You never know when you are going to find something relevant, which means it is a good idea to keep your Create the Future notebook handy to capture observations and things you hear about that can have an impact on you or your organization. It also makes sense to have Create the Future computer files to store the information you find in digital form, so you can refer back to it as necessary. Knowledge changes so rapidly that what seems relevant and useful one month might seem outdated only a short time later, or a particular article or piece of information may grow in importance based on future information searching.

If you, as Drucker did with his future-oriented mindset, keep the future dimension in your thoughts, you will be primed to seek out and find the best possible information. How you interpret and apply what you read, hear, and observe has a direct relation to discovering the future. If you adopt a future-oriented mindset, you will always be on the lookout for the conversation, the book, the article, the conference, the presentation that could become central to your future. It is a form of paying supreme attention to the opportunities and possibilities in a world of abundance.

An admirable quality of Drucker's was that he was always looking forward to his next project. He may have taken a certain amount
of pleasure and a sense of accomplishment from whatever he was
currently working on, but when it was finished, the question became,
what next? In a brief interview with the psychologist and founder
of the concept of "flow," Mihaly Csikszentmihalyi, for *Creativity*
(1996), Drucker admitted that he was a workaholic and had been
since the age of 20, and that one of the reasons for his accomplishments was "because I thrive on stress and begin to pine if there is no
deadline." When I interviewed Drucker in 2004, shortly before his
95th birthday, for an article in *USA Today*, he told me that he was
immediately looking forward to, and asking serious questions about,
his next project whenever he finished something. This exemplifies a
crucial attitude for a future-oriented mindset, and it can be applied
by anyone.

Ideally, with the help of suggestions in this chapter (and throughout the book), you will devise a program for searching out the future,
with all its potential opportunities and possibilities. You will be thinking about the Drucker future elements as you go about this work.
Being deliberate about it will increase your chances of success.

Addresses for websites referenced throughout this chapter are
listed in the Resources section of this book.

"Predicting the future can only get you into trouble. The task
is to manage what is there and to work to create what could
and should be."

—*Peter F. Drucker*, Managing in Turbulent Times, *1980*

Finding the Future

We'll focus here on two main sources for finding the future: print/online and people. This sense of discovery and possibility is geared toward, on a regular, ongoing basis, answering the question, where is the future happening? In *Managing in a Time of Great Change* (1995), Drucker wrote: "The answers to the question 'What has already happened that will make the future?' define the potential of opportunities for a given company or industry."

Similarly, in the 2004 collection *The Daily Drucker*, we find this:

> But the most important work of the executive is to identify the changes that have already happened. The important challenge in society, economics, politics, is to exploit the changes that have already occurred and to use them as opportunities. The important thing is to identify the "future that has already happened"—and to develop a methodology for perceiving and analyzing these changes.

Keeping an open mind, as Drucker did, is important. It's also worth recalling what Bruna Martinuzzi said in Chapter 1 about approaching life with the Zen concept of the beginner's mind. If we approach it the right way, there are many different possibilities for creating the future, and there are almost unlimited possibilities in what you read or hear about, or observe, to influence the future. When reviewing the material you find in sources contained in this chapter, keep in mind the potential opportunities for you, your organization, and even your profession.

Drucker discovered the future in a number of ways. He read widely, in books, newspapers, and magazines. Because of his intense interest in demographics, it is likely that he read various government reports and documents, as well as reports from individual companies and other organizations. He also learned about the future through his conversations and discussions with his wide circle of friends, consulting partners, and colleagues. But because of the increased access to information, particularly online, we have considerably more sources to choose from than Drucker did in his most active years. Let's discover and analyze more of these sources in depth.

Other People as Sources of the Future

As we mentioned in Chapter 1, Drucker was fond of the metaphor of the window; he said he looked out and observed what was visible yet often unseen by others. Because he was involved with so many different businesses, as well as educational and nonprofit groups, he had multiple windows onto the future. Besides his teaching (where he learned from his students, many of whom were experienced businesspeople in the Drucker School's Executive Management Program), he also learned about the future from his consulting partners and people he met in the course of research for his books and articles. This represented a number of viewpoints and experiences, along with a wide variety of subject matter.

To use as an example of some of his nonprofit involvement, as illustrated in Rick Wartzman's book *Drucker: A Life in Pictures* (2013), over the years he either worked with or advised a broad set of organizations, including the Girl Scouts of the USA, CARE International, American Red Cross, American Heart Association, University of Pennsylvania, Stanford Graduate Business School, Navajo Indian Tribal Council, International Rescue Committee, Japan House NYC, and Western Association of Hospitals. Then there were cultural institutions, such as the American Symphony Orchestra League, Asian Art Museum of San Francisco, Metropolitan Museum of Art, and Asian Art Council. That is a wide spectrum of people representing institutions that wanted Drucker's help in charting their future.

If you consider what this involved, it meant that he was interacting with people who thought differently, expressed different concerns, and had different views of and hopes for the future. He got to see the inner workings of organizations in how their futures were unfolding. He knew what they were working on and what their future goals were. This contributed to his knowledge base and had an impact on other areas of his life. This involvement happened when he was still consulting in the business world.

Chances are that most of us are not going to have this broad group of organizations at our disposal, but we still come in contact with lots of people, in diverse settings. If not, we can make a conscious choice to learn from more people than we interact with now, and from different types of people. We can raise the experience level and quality of our new contacts and leverage the ones we already have. What, specifically, can we learn from our friends, colleagues, and associates about the future?

The variety of these organizations (both in their missions and subject matter) helped Drucker see the crossover potential from one area to another. He was one of the first, for instance, to say that business had a lot to learn from the nonprofit world, when most people thought it was the other way around. He collected those ideas about what businesses could learn from nonprofit organizations in a 1989 article for the *Harvard Business Review,* and those ideas found expression through his work with the Peter F. Drucker Foundation for Nonprofit Management, now called the Frances Hesselbein Leadership Institute.

Hesselbein was a longtime CEO of the Girl Scouts, and Drucker worked closely with her and others in the Girl Scouts' leadership for at least a decade. When she retired, she and Bob Buford and Richard F. Schubert started the foundation, in 1990. Buford had transitioned from the for-profit world of cable television to nonprofits, and Schubert had been involved in a variety of worlds, as president of Bethlehem Steel and also president of the American Red Cross. Both had also worked with Drucker previously, when he consulted for their organizations, and they were all close friends.

As a source for the future, what activities are you involved in now that allow you to meet and interact with people who have diverse viewpoints, ideas, and experience? How might they help you see potential futures? Not all of us have access to the kinds of top leaders who were in Drucker's life, but many of us already have access to high-quality friends, family members, colleagues, and professional associates. And we can cultivate more contacts for the future, knowing that we want to sharpen our future vision.

"Balancing change and continuity requires continuous work on information."

—*Peter F. Drucker,* Management Challenges for
the 21st Century, *1999*

Human Intelligence (People and Groups)

We may not have access to the kinds of CEOs and other top-level executives that Drucker did, but we have lots of people in our lives, or those that we can add to our lives, who can be sources of information and inspiration for the future.

Besides our one-on-one interactions, we can meet in groups to focus on the future. Many of us belong to book groups or other similar interest groups that meet on a regular basis. One idea is to periodically feature books that are in some way future-oriented or could be interpreted that way. Another possibility is to form a separate future-focused book group. Listening to your fellow group members can give you valuable ideas for future endeavors, new activities, and new ways of doing things.

A journal club can help you and your work colleagues focus on the future on a regular basis. This is a long-standing tradition within the scientific and medical fields and is easily adaptable to other areas of life and work. A group of colleagues meet, perhaps at lunch once a month, to discuss in depth a particular professional journal article. This would lend itself perfectly to articles (from journals or otherwise) about the future that may have an impact on your organization. The idea can be broadened beyond your own workplace to a club of like-minded individuals in different organizations meeting to discuss an article or book that is relevant to your shared interest in the future. The sessions can be led by a moderator, though they don't have to be. They can also be done in conjunction with seminars, workshops, or similar events.

A related possibility is a discussion group about the future. This could take place at work, perhaps on a lunch hour, or after work, as a casual gathering in a restaurant or coffee shop. You could have guest speakers on occasion. In this setting, the group would not meet around a particular book, but on topics related to the future. This would be especially good for a work setting, because the topics could revolve around areas that are important to the future of your organization or your part in the organization. A great thing about meeting in a group is that you never know what you are going to hear, and since the discourse is often casual, people feel free to speak their mind.

Drucker also had lots of future-related information sent to him by friends and colleagues. Today, we are often bombarded with information sent to us by friends, colleagues, those in our profession, and others. Then there are the feeds we receive through Twitter, Facebook, LinkedIn, and related sources. Emails arrive constantly with information, links to articles, YouTube videos, and more. When looking for information about potential futures, how can you sort, limit, and filter what you are receiving?

"To make the future demands courage."

—*Peter F. Drucker,* Managing for Results, *1964*

Online and Printed Sources

With all the seemingly limitless sources, how can you really determine and recognize the future that has already happened? How can you nurture, within yourself and your colleagues, a proper mindset? By regularly scanning and reading the sources in this chapter, you will be provided with a unique perspective (because you can match it to your own experience and interest) that will help you create your future in the best possible way.

Company websites can be fruitful sources, though obviously they are mainly interested in promoting what a company is doing, including company-related blog posts. So information found on these sources is necessarily biased. Still, there can be the seeds of ideas for future projects or people with whom you'd like to meet or collaborate. We will discuss this in further detail in Chapter 4, on competitive intelligence.

Almost anything can be a source of inspiration, as we find examples of people and organizations that are doing exciting things that promise to have an impact on and importance in the future. With most of the sources listed in this chapter, there are related components, such as Twitter pages, LinkedIn and Facebook pages, and some mobile apps. A side benefit of all the reading and web surfing you do in the search for the future is that you will be better informed about the present. (See the Resources section for the addresses for each of the mentioned websites.)

"The changes that generate the future that has already happened can be found through systematic search."

—*Peter F. Drucker,* Managing for Results, *1964*

The Known Future

It is true that the future is unknown and essentially unpredictable, but there is a lot about the future that is partially known. Although you don't and can't know the details in advance, if you think about it, you'll see that there is a structure to parts of the future. For instance, your calendar tells you when you have commitments, both personal and professional. You can't know everything in advance, such as who you will meet at an event, but you know that you will be attending. The calendar is a good place to start, because it affects your availability of time: doctors' appointments, professional lunches and dinners, corporate events, conferences, classes, and more all give you a glimpse into the time you have committed in the future. Add to that tax and regulatory filings, work-related documents that must be delivered by a particular day and time, and assignments (both at work and at school), and more details of the future become known.

Newspapers often run sections on Monday about "the week ahead." Sports teams have schedules. Awards are given out or announced on a particular day. All of these involve a future where the individual, granular details are not yet known but will become known on a particular date.

If you are producing a movie, you may not win an Academy Award, but someone will, and you know when it will be awarded and what you have to do to be eligible.

Your extracurricular activities provide another source of future events. Perhaps you are giving or taking music lessons, or you are tutoring or mentoring. You might be playing in amateur sports leagues. All of these involve scheduled time and will account for a certain part of your future. Preparing for those events may be less structured but will still involve time spent.

An interesting and engrossing source of future events is *Chase's Calendar of Events*, a yearly book that has long been a staple in library collections, and which also includes an accompanying website. That is especially appropriate because the book began as a self-published phenomenon in 1957, started by the brothers Bill Chase (a newspaper librarian and journalist) and Harrison V. Chase, a university social scientist. The first edition, published in 1957 for the year 1958, was only 32 pages long with 364 entries. It has grown to the current 752 pages and more than 12,000 entries.

Chase's can be a ready source of ideas about potential futures. The subject matter is wide and eclectic: birthdays, special events/festivals, astronomical phenomena, religious observances, anniversaries, presidential proclamations, civic holidays, and so on. There is also a free website component for some daily listings.

It can also be one of the sources of information about major, ongoing events that are likely to have a variety of repercussions in the future. For instance, August 28, 2013, marked the 50th anniversary of Martin Luther King Jr.'s 'I have a dream' speech in Washington, D.C. When you know in advance of these milestones, you can plan to incorporate them into your educational and cultural activities. This could mean organizations building programs or schools designing new courses to take advantage of the unique teaching and learning opportunity.

Demographics

Auguste Comte, a 19th-century French philosopher-sociologist whom Drucker, in *The New Realities* (1989), called the "father of sociology," is credited with the saying "Demography is destiny." Drucker often cited demographic data in his work, especially about the future. In his day, most of the available sources would have been printed, and not everyone would think to delve into demographic statistics, just because they weren't widely available. Now they are available, especially online. Do you have a competitive advantage with this information? Possibly, but remember that your current and future competitors also have access to these same data.

Demographics give us the benefit of recording current and past events, with projections for the future. Where is the world heading, and what is your place in it? You can benefit and learn from government agencies, think tanks, and other organizations that have devoted considerable study on a complex topic and have made much of the information available for free. The availability of demographic statistics online represents a great advantage over what was once available only in print sources that had a limited distribution. For instance, the United Nations makes available online the *United Nations Demographic Yearbook*, which contains information about population trends, births/deaths, economics, education, housing, ethnicity, and more. A bonus of the website is that it includes previous reports, going back to 1948. These statistics can be the sources of ideas for projects, future study, and business opportunities. Reading these reports reminds us what a big and varied world we live in, and how many possibilities and opportunities there are.

A major source of demographic information for many years was the *Statistical Abstract of the United States*, compiled by the U.S. Census Bureau. However, as of October 2011, due to budget cuts, the federal government stopped compiling and aggregating these statistics in this particular format. You can still go to the abstract's website to see which individual government agencies and private organizations collect statistics. Although the abstract itself is no longer available in an updated, free form, you can still determine what is available online on the abstract's website.

The information companies ProQuest and Bernan Press have teamed up to rescue this resource and make it available to libraries and other institutions (for a fee), both in print and online.

The version of the abstract made available by ProQuest and Bernan Press contains data on births and deaths, population, the labor force, income, geography, law enforcement, science and technology, transportation, and many other categories. There is also a section of international statistics in many categories.

"The first area to examine is population. Population changes are the most fundamental—for the labor force, for the market, for social pressures, and economic opportunities."

—Peter F. Drucker, Managing for Results, *1964*

United States, Worldwide Government and Institutional Statistics

The U.S. government continues to make many other statistics available. Especially important is the information available at the Bureau of Labor Statistics website. The site offers statistics on the demographic makeup of the labor force, including age, family and marital status, and race. There is also a section on volunteering and another called *TED: The Editor's Desk*, with statistics-filled articles on many topics, including consumer expenditures, health care, productivity, and industry studies (e.g., on extended mass layoffs).The nice thing about the *TED* articles is that they come with a narrative and can be helpful for media outlets, since they provide some context to the statistics.

In addition, the U.S. government website usa.gov has a data and statistics page containing further pages, such as data.gov and the American Fact Finder, for census information. The page links to statistics from various government agencies.

The Bureau of Labor Statistics also publishes the *Occupational Outlook Handbook*. This is a great way of checking out potential employment, especially if you are thinking of switching careers. You can easily browse fastest-growing (projected) occupations, along with the highest-paying positions and careers with the most projected new jobs. You can search for occupations by category (e.g., business/ financial, health care, management, sales, and legal) and get detailed information, including median pay and education requirements. The site also has a link to a partner site called O*Net, with even more detailed information on various occupations. Included in this you'll find the types and descriptions of skills and abilities associated with a particular job (e.g., critical thinking, active listening, problem sensitivity, and deductive reasoning).

The World Bank has a wealth of statistical and demographic data and information on its website. You can check by countries, topics, and over 1,200 indicators (e.g., under Climate Change, CO_2 emissions; under Infrastructure, Container Port Traffic). It adds up to a fascinating source of ideas and inspiration, and it ideally helps to advance our understanding of the world. What game-changing ideas could you develop if you browsed these statistics on a regular basis? You may also develop an interest in and curiosity about an area of knowledge that you had never considered before. Another substantial source is the website for the International Monetary Fund (IMF), which includes the World Economic Outlook Update on trade, consumer prices, commodity prices, and growth in emerging markets and developing economies.

Besides the World Bank, IMF, and United Nations, there are many other sources for worldwide data online. For instance, the British government publishes the UK National Statistics Publication Hub. You can even get statistics (in English) on Japan from the Statistics Bureau and the Director-General for Policy Planning of Japan. An interesting compendium of world statistics comes from the independent website Worldometers. It covers world population, government, economics, food, water, health, and energy. What is especially interesting is that these statistics are added to the site in real time, so you can see the numbers rapidly flashing by when you visit its pages.

It's up to you to decide how you are going to interpret the statistics from these various sources. Some may give you a hopeful view of the world now and in the future, and some may seem more pessimistic. Some of the ideas you find may be more relevant to your professional life, rather than your personal life. You will inevitably interpret the statistics differently from someone else.

"There is a time lag between a major social, economic, or cultural event and its full impact."

—*Peter F. Drucker,* Managing for Results, *1964*

Awards, Honors, and Prizes

People and organizations that have been honored for innovations, improving the world, creating useful knowledge or products, and so on, can be terrific sources for ideas on how to create your future. Reading about these awards, and the accomplishments of the winners, can provide considerable inspiration and ideas to further your own career.

Some of the most pertinent examples are

- The Drucker Institute (Peter F. Drucker Award for Nonprofit Innovation)
- *The Economist* (Innovation Awards)
- Encore.org (Purpose Prize)
- Ernst & Young (Entrepreneur of the Year Award)
- *Financial Times*/Goldman Sachs (Business Book of the Year)
- The Frances Hesselbein Leadership Institute (Leader of the Future Award)
- John Templeton Foundation (Templeton Prize)
- MacArthur Foundation (MacArthur Fellows Program, aka "Genius Grants")
- Nobel Foundation (Nobel prizes)
- Peter Drucker Society Europe (Drucker Challenge essay contest)
- Skoll Foundation (Skoll Awards for Social Entrepreneurship)
- TED (Technology Entertainment, Design) (TED Prize)
- XPRIZE Foundation, "Revolution through Competition" (XPRIZEs)

The important thing is to study as much as possible the people and organizations that have won awards in categories in which you have an interest. You can do additional searching to find out more about their backgrounds and how they came to win the awards. Many of these are future-oriented, particularly the MacArthur Fellows awards, which in essence are meant to (very generously) fund future work by especially accomplished and promising people, individuals who, according to the MacArthur Foundation's website, have "shown extraordinary originality and dedication in their creative pursuits and a marked capacity for self-direction."

The winners of these awards can provide considerable inspiration, especially since many of them will have persevered through neglect, hard times, and rejection. You may even want to keep following their careers to see how they continue to create their futures. Most of the websites for these programs provide fairly extensive information about what the awards are, along with background on the winners.

The MacArthur fellows come from all disciplines. Even if you think you may not be interested in a particular area of work or study, it is worthwhile reading their bios and learning more about some of the fellows, most of whom have fascinating backgrounds, accomplishments, and experiences. You can't apply for one of these fellowships; instead, an anonymous group nominates candidates, and a selection committee recommends recipients.

The individual stories about the fellows provide a window into human accomplishment, potential, originality, and the sense of what is possible and what our minds can achieve. Recipients receive $500,000 payable over five years, with no strings attached. It is striking how future-oriented the awards are. The foundation explains that the fellowships are "an investment in a person's originality, insight, and potential. Indeed, the purpose of the MacArthur Fellows Program is to enable recipients to exercise their own creative instincts for the benefit of human society."

To get a sense of how eclectic the selection is, consider the backgrounds of just 5 of the 23 most recent (2012) fellows: Natalia Almada, a 37-year-old documentary filmmaker from Mexico City; Raj Chetty, a 33-year-old professor of economics at Harvard University; Olivier Guyon, a 36-year-old optical physicist and astronomer at the University of Arizona; Nancy Rabalais, a 62-year-old marine ecologist and executive director and professor at the Louisiana Universities Marine Consortium; and Benjamin Warf, a 54-year-old pediatric neurosurgeon at Boston Children's Hospital.

Most of us, of course, will not become MacArthur fellows, but we can strive to do the kind of work worthy of this kind of attention. We will explore this in more depth in Chapter 3, when we discuss how to become your own successor.

For discovering more about how some extraordinary individuals have embodied spirit and soul, many examples can be found at the website for the Templeton Prize, established by Sir John Templeton, an American-born stock investor, businessman, and philanthropist who established the prize to identify "entrepreneurs of the spirit." There you can learn more about the individual winners, to see what their paths through life have entailed, and watch many videos. It is an impressive group of names, including the most recent winners: Desmond Tutu, the former archbishop of Cape Town, South Africa, in 2013, and His Holiness the 14th Dalai Lama, in 2012. The award's website provides information on each of the winners, going back to the inaugural awardee in 1973, Mother Teresa. However, the Templeton winners are not all chosen strictly from the world of religion. In 2011 the winner was Martin J. Rees, a British theoretical astrophysicist; in 2010 it was Francisco J. Ayala, a professor of biological sciences at the University of California, Irvine, and evolutionary geneticist; and the 2009 winner was Bernard d'Espagnat, a French physicist and philosopher of science.

"I have been reading for years the acceptance speeches of Nobel prize winners."

—*Peter F. Drucker*, The Age of Discontinuity, *1969*

Higher Education Websites

If there is one place where the future is being created, it is on the campuses (and increasingly online resources) of colleges, community colleges, and universities. The leaders of tomorrow are studying there today. The subjects of tomorrow are being discussed. We can get a window into this activity by simply tracking what is going on there, and it is fairly easy to do that online. Pick a cross section of universities (both well known and otherwise) that you want to "visit" virtually on a regular basis. Look for campus activities, guest lecturers, blogs, subjects taught, profiles of professors, special events, "in the news" sections, research reports, school publications and newsletters, and more. It is a good idea to periodically scan universities that you had never heard of before or that you think you would not be interested in. It's a great way to help keep an open mind in your discovery of potential futures. You will also find out about books and other publications from professors and discover new academics whose work may hold relevance for you.

The *U.S. News & World Report* website is a great starting point for discovering sources of information on colleges and universities, for instance, MBA programs. A handy site for getting information about and links to colleges of all types is the *Forbes* top colleges list. Broaden your search even more by checking universities outside the United States. In the interest of stretching your mind and furthering your potential, it can't hurt to search for schools in areas that at first seem unfamiliar or that you think may not hold interest for you.

Here is a sample of what you can find on many higher education websites:

- News sections (covering, e.g., recent events and conferences that have been held on campus, student competitions, and information about professors who have had recent journal articles published)
- Profiles of students and professors
- University publications, including alumni magazines
- Student and faculty blogs
- Faculty awards, research, bios, publications, and expert guides
- Information about programs and classes
- Speaker series and videos
- Professors who have been quoted in the media
- Links to articles written by faculty

Besides university websites, there are online publications such as *Poets and Quants*, for MBA students and people interested in MBA-related topics. It was started by the veteran author/editor and long-time Drucker analyst John Byrne, the former editor of *BusinessWeek*, *Fast Company*, and other publications.

"We need a new concept of information and a new understanding of learning and teaching."

—*Peter F. Drucker*, The Age of Discontinuity, *1969*

Library Websites

Going back to his days as a college student in Hamburg, Germany, Drucker was an avid user of libraries. He looked at them in very practical ways, tapping into the wisdom and expertise of the librarians as to how to access the best, most relevant information. He also had a large following in the library world. He spoke to library groups on a number of occasions, including as one of the keynote speakers for the 2002 annual conference of the business-oriented Special Libraries Association, in Los Angeles.

Important sources of information beyond the free web are the normally fee-based databases many of us can tap into for free as long as we have a public library card. You can do this at home or work, without actually visiting the library. It would be interesting to think about what Drucker would make of all this readily accessible information at one's fingertips. He would have the same dilemma that we currently face, of how not to drown in data and information overload.

These library-provided databases can be a tremendous advantage in looking for future-focused information, or any type of information.

Libraries pay a considerable amount to publishers to make this information available, so it makes sense for us to take advantage of it. For instance, Gale, part of Cengage Learning, is a major publisher of directories and other materials that have been in libraries for years, but like so many other publishers, it makes much of its material (e.g., *Encyclopedia of Associations, National Organizations of the U.S.,* and *Gale Directory of Publications and Broadcast Media*) available online through participating libraries.

Many libraries also offer access to major newspapers, magazines, scholarly journals, trade journals, and more online, through the company ProQuest (the same one that helped rescue the *Statistical Abstract*). This represents high-quality information that you would be hard-pressed to find elsewhere and can be a tremendous aid in decision making about your future. Having access to this resource allows you to search through thousands of different publications, many in full text. This, and much else described in this chapter, represents an unprecedented level of access to high-quality information. It is a true revolution in how we can find information and put it to the best use. The websites of public libraries that offer this information often have explanatory guides to their databases. You can also learn more about these sources by consulting librarians in person, on the telephone, or online.

Newspapers and Magazines

Besides the newspaper and magazine availability mentioned in this chapter, there are countless media websites (many free, though more are charging for at least some of their content). It is undeniable that Drucker derived considerable value from the heavy amount of reading he did. One of the most interesting regular features on the Drucker Institute website is the weekly "What (We Think) Drucker Would Be Reading." Obviously, that is speculation, but everyone has to decide what to read, not just for daily information and inspiration, but for guidance on how to advance into the future.

Most people probably have their favorites for online and print reading. Beyond the specialist publications that you follow for your work or areas of study, you can learn a lot from such publications/ websites as *Bloomberg Businessweek, The Economist, Fast Company, Financial Times, Forbes, Fortune, The Futurist, Los Angeles Times, MIT Sloan Management Review, MIT Technology Review, New York Times, Time, U.S. News & World Report, Washington Post,* and *Wired*. Reading/ skimming at least some of these titles on a regular basis will help you cast a wide net for potential futures.

Some have published future-themed sections, such as *Fortune*'s Future Issue, from January 2013, detailing the exploits of Google CEO Larry Page and the hospital operating room robotics efforts of companies like Intuitive Surgical. When *USA Today* turned 30 years old in September 2012, it published a special feature: "USA TOMORROW: Leaders Foresee a Fascinating Future World," interviewing a number of "visionaries" about where they see the world going in their various spheres of influence 30 years in the future, in 2042. These included James Cameron, director of the films *Avatar* and *Titanic*; Andrés Duany, the cofounder and guru of the New Urbanism movement in city planning; and Marc Andreessen, the online pioneer cofounder of Netscape, who is now a venture capitalist.

Andreessen was also on the cover of a special 2012 issue of *Wired*, for an extended Q&A, "The Man Who Makes the Future." That accompanied a long feature story, "How to Spot the Future." Seven rules for spotting the future are identified and explained (e.g., looking for "cross-pollinators," "liberators," and "time wasters"), accompanied by illuminating sidebars with visionaries such as Joi Ito, director of the MIT Media Lab, Internet pioneer Vint Cerf, venture capitalist Esther Dyson, technology forecaster Paul Saffo, and publisher Tim

O'Reilly. As mentioned in Chapter 1, both Dyson and Saffo joined Drucker in writing about the future in the *Harvard Business Review*'s 75th anniversary issue, in 1997.

Drucker was a big fan in particular of *The Economist* and wrote two extended features about the world ahead, in 1989 and 2001, for that publication. He was a serious reader of it, and he'd appreciate the extended availability on the publication's website. The weekly magazine (although it refers to itself as a newspaper) is a gold mine of information about business, technology, culture, politics, and more, with coverage around the world. It is really an indispensable source for keeping up with what is important worldwide, with uniformly excellent writing. For future-oriented material, see in particular the *Technology Quarterly*, which covers all aspects of technology, including the computer world, medicine, the sciences, the environment, transportation, and energy. Each edition features "Brain Scan," an interview with a technology innovator.

The Economist also publishes the yearly *The World in ...* series, which now has an extensive website. (Drucker also contributed an article, "Can e-Commerce Deliver?" to *The World in 2000*.) Along with the many predictions for the next 12 months and the possible effects of those events, you can benefit from the well-organized thoughts and opinions by subject experts and high-profile practitioners from business, technology, the arts, politics, health care, and other fields, putting into context information about what lies ahead.

This publication is valuable because it shows you what people and organizations are planning to do in the coming year, not just offering speculation but also solid plans and evidence. The website archives past issues, going back to 2004, although the print issues go back at least 25 years. The book *Megachange: The World in 2050*, edited by Daniel Franklin, executive editor of *The Economist* and editor of *The World in ...*, was published in 2012.

Broadcast/Cable Websites

In addition to television and radio, media organizations in this sphere often have significant web presences, with additional audio, video, and graphics, plus accompanying articles. To learn more, check the websites of such organizations as the BBC, CNBC, CNN, CBC, and NPR.

The BBC, in particular, has a section of its website devoted to the future, which covers international science, technology, the environment, and health. CNN has a similar site, What's Next, about innovation, culture, and social change.

Organizations and Think Tanks

A logical place to look for hints to the future is on the websites of organizations, consultancies, special initiatives, and think tanks that make it their business to learn more about the future. This brief list is meant to show just some of the possibilities:

- Accenture (Public Service for the Future)
- Burson-Marsteller (Future Perspective)
- Deloitte (Center for the Edge)
- Foresight (future-oriented organization from the British government)
- Future Leaders in Philanthropy
- The Future of Work (an initiative from Lynda Gratton, a professor at the London Business School)
- The Future of Work (the research and advisory firm founded by former Harvard Business School professor Jim Ware)
- futurethink
- Insight Labs
- Institute for the Future (IFTF)

- McKinsey & Company (The Future of Work in Advanced Economies)
- Pew Research Center (especially for social trends, as well as a source of demographic data)
- PSFK Labs (future-oriented consulting company)
- RAND Corporation
- World Future Society (WFS)

In addition, it can be worth following organizations that are not completely future-focused, but that do important work related to the future, such as AARP, Aspen Institute, Booz & Co., and Booz Allen Hamilton.

Organizations such as the IFTF and the WFS (slogan: "Tomorrow is built today") focus their mission on studying, understanding, preparing for, and planning for the future.

Although it is true that Drucker believed that predicting the future was a waste of time, these organizations deal more in forecasts and thinking seriously about the future based on present problems and innovations. That is fairly close to what Drucker himself did. And Drucker's article "The Future That Has Already Happened," which originally appeared in 1997 in the *Harvard Business Review*, was reprinted in *The Futurist*, the magazine published by the WFS. The magazine runs interviews with thought leaders such as Stephen Wolfram, founder of Wolfram Alpha, and the inventor/entrepreneur/visionary Ray Kurzweil, and features about people and organizations involved in efforts to create a better future for everyone.

What matters is to focus less on the predictions or even the forecasting aspects of the information and more on the present-day thinking that goes behind it. In addition, you can learn more about the people seeking to help society find its best possible expression in the future. The visionary writer/inventor Arthur C. Clarke (who wrote the short story that was the basis for the film *2001: A Space Odyssey*) was a longtime active member of the WFS and was interviewed for *The Futurist* shortly before his death. The WFS also has an enlightening series available in pdf form, "2020 Visionaries," with essays for the next decade by future-oriented thought leaders on such topics as open source drug manufacturing, nanorobotics, technology, education, the media, spirituality, engineering, sustainability, and climate change.

The IFTF is a nonprofit research organization that has a 44-year-plus history of working with companies, universities, and other organizations, described on its website as "helping all kinds of organizations make the futures they want." This emphasis on making and creating is perfectly in line with Drucker's thoughts, even if he was lukewarm about forecasting itself. The organization looks at technology, health, food, gaming, manufacturing, and the future of work, as well as the future of education, through research, conferences, and publications.

Bob Johansen of the IFTF has written an excellent book, *Leaders Make the Future,* about actively creating the future, rather than merely reacting to it. And one of the superstars of the online games world, Jane McGonigal (author of *Reality Is Broken: Why Games Make Us Better and How They Can Change the World*), is now part of the organization. The IFTF website has a considerable amount of useful information, including many colorful, highly informative maps of different topics, such as an "Ecosystems of Well-Being" map. The active, creation aspect of the IFTF is particularly intriguing, taking the information presented (or being involved in its presentation) and then using it to make a better-informed, well-intentioned future, both individually and organizationally. The organization's work on the future is captured in a beautifully designed map, "History of the Future."

It's also worth reading some of the work of the many thoughtful futurists who can help spark ideas for the types of work you'd like to accomplish. Whether or not you agree with everything they have to say, the best provide food for thought that can help serve as a valuable guide as you discover the future that has already happened. That is because the best of their work is based on what is known of currently available work and technology, and what types of work and initiatives that visionaries are currently doing. In this category are authors/practitioners such as Kurzweil (whose latest book is *How to Create a Mind: The Secret of Human Thought Revealed*), Johansen, Daniel Burrus (*Flash Foresight: How to See the Invisible and Do the Impossible*), Cecily Sommers (*Think Like a Futurist*), Don Tapscott (*Wikinomics: How Mass Collaboration Changes Everything*), Joel Barker (*Paradigms: The Business of Discovering the Future*), Peter Schwartz (*The Art of the Long View: Planning for the Future in an Uncertain World*), and Alvin Toffler (*Future Shock*). (As a corrective, there is no shortage of books that contend futurism is bunk; in particular, see *Future Babble*, by Dan Gardner, a Canadian journalist.)

In Chapter 3, we'll look more closely at some of the people who always seem to be ahead of the curve, creating the future for themselves and others and, in some cases, actively making their own forecasts.

"But what about future trends and events we are not even aware of yet? If there is one thing that can be forecast with confidence, it is that the future will turn out in unexpected ways."

—*Peter F. Drucker,* Managing in the Next Society, *2002*

Conclusion

A good Drucker-related combination of ideas to keep in mind for looking for the future is keep an open mind + cast a wide net + figure out what's relevant. The combination of print/online sources plus human intelligence from your face-to-face meetings with groups and individuals can provide powerful insights for the future.

Keep thinking of the Drucker mindset, where consideration of the future is always in your mind as you read, listen, discuss, and observe. Note the things that do not fit with what you already know, but that could lead to significant changes for you, your profession, or your organization. Try to decide how much time you would like to spend daily or weekly in this search for the future. Keep your printed and/or online notebooks and files ready for relevant information, and flag the items you want to track.

Try for as much balance as possible in your future searching. For instance, balance the time you spend searching for demographics or other government-related data online with material from newspapers/magazines or from higher education websites. Keep a good record of how many ideas have been generated that can lead to a brighter future. Keep thinking of your process for the future, and how you can make it as personal and meaningful to you as possible.

In Chapter 3, we'll look at how you can start applying what you are discovering and learning about the future to thinking about getting the most out of your work, by thinking of yourself as your own successor.

Chapter Review

In this chapter we have looked at the wide range of sources (in human contact, as well as in print and online) that can have an effect on your future, in particular, in your identification of the future that has already happened. We've outlined specific sources for demographic information, one of Drucker's key drivers of the future. News and media sites have been identified as important sources, as have websites for government statistics and websites for institutions of higher learning.

The importance of face-to-face contacts has been emphasized, through various groups and the possibility for focused study in journal clubs. We have also seen how learning more about the winners of various awards and prizes shows us what the human spirit can achieve, while providing inspiration for our own journeys.

The possibilities for learning about the future are endless. This chapter has provided information (with links to websites in the Resources section at the back of the book) that will provide inspiration and food for thought on your continued journey. If you follow the suggestions here, you are bound to not only have a better future, but also, in the Drucker spirit, be well informed and future ready.

Checklist

✓ Have your Creating the Future notebook and/or computer file ready to capture information from your searches in the sources above, as well as what you learn from other people.

✓ Take a quick tour of as many of the websites mentioned in this chapter as you can, to give you an idea of the scope of future-related material online.

✓ Check with your public library about special databases available to you.

✓ If you are not already in a group that can be adapted for future-related discussions, consider starting one, and think of potential members.

✓ Consider the idea of starting or joining a journal club.

BECOME YOUR OWN SUCCESSOR

3

Where do you see yourself at 95? That is not an unreasonable question these days. Peter Drucker lived until eight days before his 96th birthday, in 2005, and he was productive until nearly the end of his life. When I interviewed him at the Drucker Archives in Claremont, California, in April 2005, I brought up the notion of his being such an important role model to 21st-century knowledge workers. I mentioned that just in the year leading up to our interview, his book *The Daily Drucker,* which became one of his most popular works, was released, and he had been published in the *Wall Street Journal, Harvard Business Review, Foreign Affairs,* and elsewhere. That high-profile, highly productive output would be tough for writers of any age, let alone someone in his mid-90s. It was truly a testament to the power of productive aging, without, as he had put it earlier "becoming a prisoner of the past." That he produced so much in less than a year is truly remarkable.

In 2011, six years after Drucker's death, the Brazilian management magazine *Administradores* asked me who, if anyone, could be considered his successor as the top management authority. While considering various possibilities, I raised the possibility of "Drucker as His Own Successor." While this may seem flippant, I was completely serious. His work has become understood in different ways, because so much has been written about him, in books, articles, and online, from so many different sources in recent years. We also have much greater access to his work via the Internet. In addition, books by him were released posthumously. This provides an added level of understanding and allows us to read his work with renewed intensity.

Indeed, Drucker became his own successor during his lifetime, as he remained atop the lists of management theorists over a period of many years. I believe that we can look to his career for a guide as to how we, too, can become and remain our own successors.

Becoming your own successor is somewhat metaphorical and shouldn't be taken literally. It requires a stretch of the imagination. Some possible interpretations of this concept include something fairly straightforward, such as a promotion within your current organization. But it also may mean staying in your current job but redefining and reinventing it. Rather than your organization hiring someone else to do your reconfigured job, a somewhat "different version" of you is hired/retained. It also may mean that you eventually leave your job for something better, more suitable, or different. Think of athletes who break their own record as another useful metaphor.

Applying the Drucker Example

How can you harness and apply Drucker's example in your own life? How can you create your own future? The reality is that many of us live or soon will live in a world where our professional identity is defined by an ongoing portfolio of creative output rather than a job title.

This chapter deals with self-development in the service of creating your future, so you can continually strive to think of yourself as your own successor. A big component is improving your life and how you work and cultivating your sense of excellence. It means thinking more entrepreneurially and more creatively. By applying the Drucker mindset, where the future is always somewhere in your consciousness, you are thinking of the kinds of transitions and transformations you need to make to improve your life. If you hope to live a long life, as Drucker did, you need to decide, deliberately, the nature and direction of your work.

Drucker worked all along, learning, meeting, and interacting with people, and building on his own work as a writer, consultant, and teacher. He always tried to tap into the best information and best expertise. His output and dedication were a testament to shunning complacency with one's own work and reputation.

"The first priority for one's own development is to strive for excellence."

—*Peter F. Drucker,* Managing the Non-Profit Organization, *1990*

Here are some key ways that you can cultivate the actions and abilities, based on Drucker's example, to become your own successor:

- **Diversify your efforts and outputs.** Drucker wrote books and articles on a regular basis, in a wide variety of outlets. People who have not seen his articles in the *Harvard Business Review* or *Forbes* may have encountered them in publications with a somewhat different readership, such as the *Atlantic* and, in earlier years, the *Saturday Evening Post*. He also reached people through different but related activities, consulting, and teaching.
- **Develop a powerful personal brand.** He may not have liked the terminology, but Drucker's name continues to stand for something, especially when it comes to the study of management. There is tremendous name recognition, and equally important, that name/brand is synonymous with quality and high standards.

- **Maintain a global outlook and worldview.** During the 2005 interview, Drucker told me that a crucial necessity for today's knowledge worker was a global worldview. He wrote for a worldwide audience, and his books were published in more than 30 languages. It is impressive to look at the bookshelves at the Drucker Archives to see the sheer volume of the translations of his books. He also lectured and consulted worldwide and maintained his serious interest in Japanese art. He was a collector and expert, even teaching the subject during the 1980s at Pomona College. As distances shrink, more of our work has the potential to take on a worldwide reach. In this way, we can learn from artists, architects, and musicians, many of whom have international outlets for their work. A global worldview in these fields has been a given for many years.

- **Remain relevant.** As we age, we have to figure out ways to remain relevant to people of all ages, especially younger ones. This expresses itself in the workplace when we have a number of generations working together and increasingly younger people managing older workers. Drucker did what was necessary as he aged to make his work relevant, so there was a consistent demand for his output as a writer, consultant, and teacher into his 90s.

- **Produce a consistently impressive body of work.** The cumulative effect of the quantity and quality of Drucker's work is impressive. The sheer number of books and articles is a testament to his work ethic and desire to create lasting ideas. We can look to his example to continue building our own body of work, whether or not that work is creative in nature.

- **Create work that benefits others.** One reason Drucker's work remains so influential, is that it was predicated on helping others. His work revolved around helping others to become successful and to understand themselves and their work more fully.

His consulting helped executives improve the operations of their organizations and guided them to think more clearly about their work. His writing was a beacon of wisdom to millions and remains so. His books continue to help people lead more productive lives inside and outside the workplace. And his teaching aided countless students over the years to become more effective and accomplished.

Knowledge workers who excel in today's challenging environment are generative and through their efforts and output help others create their futures and improve their lives. We'll look at how Drucker and other people have exemplified these concepts and how you can build them into your own self-development. We will also examine inner strength tools, such as working smarter, thriving, self-efficacy, awareness, attention, and mindfulness.

The application of the Drucker mindset for the future implies change, movement, transition, and transformation. It requires not being satisfied or complacent. Keeping the future in mind will affect how you make decisions both on a day-to-day basis and long-term. You may consider changing jobs or professions or starting new educational endeavors. Uncertainty should be factored into your decisions. You will never have 100 percent certainty, or anything near it, but you can still act and plan accordingly, accepting the opportunity and challenge that the future is yours to create.

"Self-development may require learning new skills, new knowledge, and new manners."

—*Peter F. Drucker,* Management, *revised edition, 2008*

In the 2005 interview, I asked Drucker about areas of surprise in his long career. He told me that

> my greatest success has been in Japan, and it totally surprised me.... My ... absence of success [in Europe], if you look at the enormous length of time it took before the Europeans paid any attention, not just to me but to my areas of concern, greatly surprised me, took forever.... I've had a much greater impact on nonprofits than I've had on businesses. And though I have been active in nonprofits for a long time, [that] surprised me. ... I have learned that one plans, one has to plan, but one also [should] know that events [can] be contrary.

A Brief Tour of Drucker's Self-Management for the Future

While there is no need to go into everything about Drucker's attitudes toward self-management here, a few words are in order on how his views on this subject relate to the future. Because we live longer (indeed, many people can expect to outlive their places of work), Drucker, believed that self-management was a necessity. You—and not the organization for which you work—hold the responsibility for your career, the learning that bolsters that career, your future advancement, and other important life decisions.

This means you should focus your efforts on meaningful results that benefit not just you but also your organization and other people. You should also get your priorities in order, based on your personal values and think about how you can make a positive difference. That provides a solid basis for how you'd like your career to develop.

Self-management means aiming for contribution and effectiveness, not just efficiency. Organizing your time becomes an important issue, which we will cover later in this chapter. The same goes for lifelong learning. Drucker felt that knowledge workers often learn the most when they are teaching. This requires looking for opportunities to teach within the workplace, or to do volunteer teaching such as at Sunday school, or perhaps to become an adjunct professor at a local university. A major focus of self-management is building on strengths rather than weaknesses, while not ignoring the latter. All of these future-oriented areas require serious reflection, one of the key elements of the Drucker future mindset.

You can learn more about these topics in my first book, *Living in More Than One World: How Peter Drucker's Wisdom Can Inspire and Transform Your Life*, published in 2009, and in the chapter "Managing Oneself" from Drucker's book *Management Challenges for the 21st Century*. His classic, *The Effective Executive*, is outstanding. The 2006 paperback reissue includes an introduction, "What Makes an Effective Executive?," which originally appeared as an article in the June 2004 *Harvard Business Review*.

It is important to note that Drucker advocated diversifying your life. This relates to areas such as volunteering and working with non-profits, as well as having outside interests that are fun yet serious and rewarding. We will discuss further in Chapter 5.

Inner Strength Tools for the Future-Focused Mindset

If the future is indeed a mindset, then we require various tools of inner strength to help us think and act better on our journey. These tools will help us use our minds most effectively and creatively, and will be a key component in how you can become your own successor.

How we use our mind is crucial to our success as individuals and within organizations. This was underscored on April 2, 2013, when President Barack Obama announced the $100 million government-sponsored BRAIN (Brain Research through Advancing Innovative

Neurotechnologies) initiative that will map the human brain. "Ideas are what power our economy," President Obama said. "When we invest in the best ideas before anybody else does, our businesses and our workers can make the best products and deliver the best services before anybody else."

Let's take a closer look at such tools as mindfulness, the relaxation response, and self-efficacy.

Mindfulness as an Aid to Excellence

One of the best tools for considering your future is mindfulness. Much of the discussion on the role of mindfulness has been led by Jeremy Hunter, an assistant professor at the Drucker School. I first became friends with him in 2002, on my initial visit to Claremont to begin researching *Living in More Than One World*. He was already teaching at the school then, helping students manage themselves, in part through the structured, focused use of meditation. At the same time, he was working in the Quality of Life Center with the famed psychologist Mihaly Csikszentmihalyi, author of *Flow: The Psychology of Optimal Experience*. Csikszentmihalyi had recently moved to the Drucker School after teaching for many years at the University of Chicago.

During the ensuing years, the world has caught up with Hunter's focus on self-management, especially the management of attention through mindfulness. His work has filtered into the mass media, as reported on NPR and articles in the *Los Angeles Times* and the *Wall Street Journal*. In 2010 he and Scott Scherer contributed a chapter, "Knowledge Worker Productivity and the Practice of Self-Management," to *The Drucker Difference*.

I sat in on one of Hunter's classes at the Drucker School in 2005. And at Drucker Day 2012, when Drucker School alumni and friends gathered for their annual day of networking and education, I attended a class in which he led a session called "Cultivating Your Resources: Building Resilience from the Inside Out."

He explained that as we try to function in today's hyperconnected, incredibly busy world, we often experience stress levels that are too high, accompanied by potentially harmful, unsustainable lifestyles. In the large classroom, he led us in a brief meditation, while we remained in our seats. It involved ways we could discover internal resources, such as recalling positive experiences, favorite places, or pieces of music, and external ones, such as values, beliefs, and experiences that sustain and nourish us.

Doing this communally, even in a group of people that would likely never get together again, was powerful and moving. For me, and for many others, briefly reflecting and paying attention to these inner resources produced positive changes in both body and mind. We can practice this on our own or look for guiding spirits in classes offered in communities and sometimes in workplaces.

In *The Drucker Difference*, Hunter writes: "Mindfulness practices are a method of attention development that enhances self-awareness, self-regulation and self-transformation." He built a practice of self-management based on his research study of prominent people who practice mindfulness. He found that it had all sorts of benefits for physical and mental health, especially stress reduction. Hunter has built these practices into his own life as a consultant, researcher, and professor, and he says that they were instrumental in his overcoming a diagnosis of a terminal illness when he was 20. He says that he was told then that he had a 90 percent chance of dying within 5 years, yet he's "outlived that prognosis by decades."

Hunter's teaching helps students guard against automaticity, or automatic behavior, which refers to making decisions on autopilot, based on routine and how things have always been done. By acting mindfully, in the moment, you can overcome preconceptions and choose the most appropriate response to any given situation.

Mindfulness has caught on with the employees of Google, which offers a course called "Search Inside Yourself." The executive who began the course, Chade-Meng Tan, has now started the Search Inside Yourself Leadership Institute, reaching out to other companies, and has written a best-selling book, *Search Inside Yourself: The Unexpected Path to Achieving Success, Happiness (and World Peace)* (2012). Target, General Mills, Facebook, and Twitter offer similar courses. Bill George, the retired chairman and CEO of Medtronic, is also a major proponent of mindfulness, in his writing, blogging, and teaching at the Harvard Business School.

In an article for the inaugural (April 2013) issue of *Mindful* magazine, Hunter briefly outlines a number of practices that can help with challenges many of us face in the workplace. For instance, when you are feeling physically worn down and find yourself mindlessly staring at your computer screen, take a moment for a "full-body scan," noting the sensations in your body at that particular time, then go outside and breathe some fresh air. Another suggestion: when you are stuck on a particularly tricky problem, try to sit for five minutes without doing anything. Hunter then recommends you contemplate the problem as if it were the first time you were encountering it.

Mindfulness can be done with or without meditation. You can also build the practice of mindfulness into work and play or when walking and driving, concentrating on the task at hand and trying to not be bothered by distractions.

Mindfulness and the Relaxation Response

Mindfulness meditation is one way of eliciting the "relaxation response," the title of a 1975 multimillion-selling book about a technique for concentration and stress reduction by Herbert Benson, at the time a Harvard

Medical School cardiologist. Because of his influence and longevity, Benson has become a Drucker-like figure in his field. He is still active in researching and writing about holistic health, including variations of the relaxation response, as the director emeritus of the Benson-Henry Institute for Mind Body Medicine at Massachusetts General Hospital. He has also done considerable work with corporations.

Relaxation in this sense does not mean engagement in relaxing activities, but rather the response of the body to techniques that, among other things, decrease heart rate, breath rate, and blood pressure and provide an alternative to the "fight or flight" response. Although many of the stressors of life today are similar to what they were in 1975, when the relaxation response was introduced, a stressor that did not really exist then is our 24/7 always-on, always-connected, always-expected-to-be-available culture.

Meditation (mindfulness meditation and other varieties) is one vehicle that can be used to elicit the response, but there are others, including yoga, repetitive prayer, and even activities like knitting and crocheting. There can be a religious or spiritual component to the response, but it is not necessary. There are sources available online and in Benson's books to learn more about the relaxation response and how to elicit it. See if any of these suggestions can add to your techniques for developing the inner, underlying strengths that will help you improve your life, both inside and outside the workplace.

Self-Efficacy

Drawing on inner strength and courage is a component of Albert Bandura's powerful concept of self-efficacy. Bandura, a Stanford University psychology professor emeritus, counts as another Drucker-like figure. He is one of the most cited social scientists of all time in the scholarly literature and is highly influential in psychology, education, and related fields. In his mid-80s, he is still active and in demand, even if he no longer teaches regularly.

Self-efficacy falls within Bandura's social cognitive theory, one of his major achievements. In an entry he wrote for the *Corsini Encyclopedia of Psychology*, he describes self-efficacy in this way: "Perceived self-efficacy is concerned with people's beliefs in their ability to influence events that affect their lives. This core belief is the foundation of human motivation, performance accomplishments, and emotional well-being."

This goes beyond confidence. It is the belief that we can take on a task and make it work. As Bandura explains it, this concept builds on a series of successes, of what he calls personal mastery, which can then be applied or used as motivation in other areas. It requires perseverance and resilience. It also requires what he calls "social modeling," seeing people who are somewhat similar to you who have succeeded. An aspect of self-efficacy is "social persuasion," or the signals and motivations you get from other people. Bandura believes that another way of "altering self-efficacy beliefs is to enhance physical strength and stamina, reduce stress and depression, and correct misinterpretations of somatic states." As you can see from these various components of self-efficacy, there must be a reasonable chance of success in an endeavor, more than just confidence, as important as that may be.

Five Minds for the Future

Harvard educational psychologist and author Howard Gardner is known for his theory of multiple intelligences. Although it has remained somewhat controversial and even disputed, the idea that IQ scores don't necessarily reflect our intelligence accurately has become a powerful concept for many people in a variety of fields.

Gardner also has built considerable credibility in the business world and elsewhere through such books as *Leading Minds* (1995) and *Creating Minds* (1993). Of interest for our purposes is a construct detailed in his 2007 book, *Five Minds for the Future*, of the different types of mind frames we all must develop to navigate the future:

1. The **disciplined** mind shows how to apply oneself to the task at hand, whether in the workplace, in school, or other contexts. This fits well with Bandura's theory of self-efficacy.
2. The **synthesizing** mind is centered on how to incorporate, understand, and evaluate information from different sources and be able to explain it to others.
3. The **creating** mind thinks differently, questions differently, and goes into unfamiliar territory. Optimistically, Gardner says that this type of mind "seeks to remain at least one step ahead of even the most sophisticated computers and robots." (This may be wishful thinking in the not-too-distant future.) Gardner cites Drucker's management work in his chapter on this type of mind, along with the art of Pablo Picasso, the writing of James Joyce, and the music of Duke Ellington.
4. The **respectful** mind fosters tolerance and the ability to work with and understand people unlike oneself. Drucker's ideas of getting beyond one's four walls (and comfort zone), to meet and interact with new people, are particularly applicable here.
5. The **ethical** mind requires us to think beyond our own interests and needs to that of a wider community and society. It asks how we can improve not just our own lives but the lives of others.

Reflect on how these different minds amplify Drucker's thoughts on self-management and how they can relate to your career goals and becoming your own successor. How closely do these descriptions match up with the way you now think? How could you think differently to consciously incorporate them for your journey into the future?

"One can never be sure what the knowledge worker thinks— and yet thinking is his specific work; it is his 'doing.'"

—*Peter F. Drucker,* The Effective Executive, *1967*

Thriving at Work

To create our best futures, we must consider how we can go beyond surviving to thriving at work. We must seek to identify areas in which we excel. Christine Porath, Gretchen Spreitzer, and their coauthors tackled this issue in the article "Thriving at Work: Toward Its Measurement, Construct Validation, and Theoretical Refinement," in the *Journal of Organizational Behavior* in 2011. This is part of the work in a field known as positive organizational scholarship, at the University of Michigan Ross School of Business, where Spreitzer teaches.

I interviewed Spreitzer for a short feature, "The Importance of Happiness in the Workplace," in *Leader to Leader* in 2012. The research by Spreitzer, Porath, and their colleagues showed that people thrive at work when they showed a sense of vitality or energy, Spreitzer told me. She said this was related to happiness, as they were similarly positive emotions. However, this went beyond the latter, since it conveyed a sense of growth, of improving and getting better at what you do. This has direct implications for improving life in the present, for the benefit of the future.

Spreitzer related some areas in which people thrive more at work that are congruent with Drucker's outlook, such as if they were learning, could find meaning in their work, and were helping other people. To think properly so you can thrive, Spreitzer suggested that people should eat a well-balanced diet, which includes high-protein snacks, get enough sleep, and take breaks during the day. All of these things seem like common sense, yet how often are they ignored? Besides practicing the discipline yourself, if you are a manager or leader, you should try to help others thrive and grow as well.

Challenges and Opportunities for Learning in the 21st Century

In the 2005 interview, Drucker told me that "knowledge work … is just beginning to be affected by new technology and overall by new concepts. And that's the great frontier of the next … 50 years. It is predictable that in 30 or 50 years knowledge work, especially teaching, the biggest area of knowledge work, will be radically different from anything it has ever been. The effective executive of tomorrow will have to make knowledge work effective, productive."

I asked him if the newness of the tools and the technology is one reason that it's so difficult to organize information and to make it productive. He replied:

> In … the past, there was very little information, and what there was, was primarily about the inside of the organization. Accounting began really as a discipline, not so very long ago, the end of the nineteenth century … as that's when it changed from being an adding machine to an information machine. And that has made a tremendous difference. But that's inside. The really important things for an organization happen on the outside. That information is beginning to be organized … on the Internet especially, and that will make a tremendous difference.

Drucker challenges us to focus on opportunities rather than problems, as well as to consider change as opportunity. I asked him if an opportunity for people to function effectively in the future is to organize information effectively. He replied:

It's beginning to, yes. There are a few areas in which it's moving very fast. You know, I began my career working in a bank. Banks, banking have been transformed by information. The end product is the same, pretty much, but the process is totally different. Most other areas are beginning [to change]. It is the availability of information [that's changed], [not] the concept of information. And we are moving into a knowledge society based on information technology, and that's new. Now, lawyers and physicians have for a long time had organized information; the rest of us had tidbits.

Besides the "new" or even "urgent" information, there is simply too much information already available to be properly digested. It goes beyond information overload. There is no way we can master what is already available to us, online and in print. We'll never go to enough conferences, take enough classes, learn from enough other people to make up for it. We have to come up with our own strategies to avoid overload and the resulting burnout and anxiety.

Ongoing Education

One of Drucker's defining statements about the future is found in *Managing for Results* (1964). Over the course of the ensuing 40 years, he also placed emphasis on a combination of education and personal dedication to make possible a bright future.

This was in evidence in his commencement address to the University of Scranton, in Scranton, Pennsylvania, my hometown, on May 31, 1964. I was a young boy at the time and would not have known who Drucker was, yet his words would hold significant meaning for me later in life.

He spoke that day of how people must transform their lives on an ongoing basis, as the world is continually changing, requiring different work and different knowledge as people further their lives and careers. He told the graduates (who are of retirement age now) that they had a responsibility to put their knowledge to work for the benefit of others, not just for themselves. Commencement addresses are naturally future-focused, and Drucker did not disappoint while demanding much from these young people about to start a new chapter in their lives. He reminded them that it wasn't long ago that most people left school at 14 to go to work, and that the graduates' years of education up to that point represented sacrifices from parents and money from taxpayers—and that only time and results would tell if that money had been spent wisely. He called them the first generation of the "knowledge revolution."

Drucker touched on familiar themes from his books of that period: the change from producing and manufacturing tangible objects to knowledge work; the relatively recent demand for educated people; how teaching hadn't changed much in hundreds of years. "But what education and knowledge mean to society," he said, "that has changed drastically, and within the lifetime of the older generation still living."

He reminded them that power and influence should not be used for selfish ends. They and other new graduates elsewhere faced "a very much brighter future than young people have ever faced before." He then issued this challenge, which remains applicable for any knowledge worker living today: "I hope you will remember that in turn it is your responsibility to put your knowledge and your education to work where they produce the most—for you, for your families, for your society, for your country, and for mankind."

Drucker believed that education never ended for a successful knowledge worker. Fortunately, we have innumerable options to increase our learning, many more than when Drucker was most active. In Chapter 2 we discussed monitoring the websites of colleges and universities as a way of seeing how the future is unfolding. In the spirit of self-development, you may want to take this one step further to seek new educational paths for yourself. This can play out in many ways:

- Enroll in in-house training at work or a more formal corporate program
- Take massive open online courses (MOOCs), mostly free and mostly nondegree courses from Harvard, Stanford, and elsewhere, via such companies as Coursera, Udacity, and edX
- Take one or more courses at a time at a local college, university, or community college
- Take courses from government-related organizations, such as the Small Business Administration
- Audit or take free or low-cost courses at your alma mater
- Take classes or pursue degrees online at universities outside your geographical area (including through for-profit, predominantly online schools, e.g., University of Phoenix and DeVry University)
- Enroll in lifelong learning or personal enrichment programs, such as Odyssey, offered by Johns Hopkins University and other schools
- Discover informal learning through TED videos, available online, and attend a TEDx session in your area, if offered

---

"I think the growth industry in this country and the world will soon be continuing education for adults."

—*Peter F. Drucker*, Managing in a Time of Great Change, *1995*

The Crucial Role of Community Colleges

President Obama has made community colleges a centerpiece of many of his economic programs and has tied their success to the future success of the American economy, and of the country's competitiveness in the unforgiving world economy. Drucker held a similar view about the potential of these schools.

Community colleges are in many ways the unsung (and under-appreciated) heroes of American education. They have the potential to make a difference in the lives of many people, but especially those who come from immigrant families or families where the student is the first person to attend college. They offer lower-cost alternatives to people who are struggling in the economic downturn, as well as pathways to four-year schools and beyond.

It's true that these schools have their own issues and challenges, such as low graduation rates and varying levels of student success, retention, and persistence rates (students who stay in school, or persist from one semester or school year to the next). But it is also true that many of the students have personal and/or family challenges that other students do not. These include going to school part time while holding down one or more jobs to support a family, child care burdens, heavy financial need, and taking classes at night and on weekends.

Yet these schools provide a tremendous number of good opportunities and can be an integral part of the future for many. Taking classes or getting a degree at a community college can help you change careers, reinvent yourself, learn new subjects, meet new people, learn new languages, and more.

If you yourself don't require any of those things, you may still be able to help by initiating public-private partnerships with local community colleges on behalf of your organization or business. Many of these schools now have these types of vital partnerships among nonprofits, universities, and businesses. This is especially true for retraining workers and providing opportunities in nursing and other health care fields. Community colleges can be ideal places to start job-training programs, internships, or apprenticeships. They are ideal for the burgeoning world of health information technology/health information management, and many have a strong focus on getting students ready for careers in the so-called STEM (science, technology, engineering, and mathematics) subjects.

Collaborations between community colleges and local businesses can help to create your personal future and that of your organization, but they also can help create the future for students. Organizations such as the Lumina Foundation have been engaged in fruitful partnerships with community colleges for years. The Bill and Melinda Gates Foundation has been a vital supporter. What role might community colleges play in your life?

"The community college was actually designed ... to educate technologists who have both the needed theoretical knowledge and the manual skill. On this, I am convinced, rests both the still huge productivity advantage of the American economy and the ... American ability to create, almost overnight, new and different industries."

—*Peter F. Drucker,* Management Challenges for
the 21st Century, *1999*

Working Smarter: Support Tools, for Transformation

I'm always on the lookout for people who offer valuable tools and techniques to help others work smarter and more effectively. I asked some of them for their ideas on ways that today's knowledge workers could best navigate the future.

William Reed was born in the United States but has lived in Japan for many years. He has a varied career as a consultant, speaker, teacher, trainer, martial artist, and writer. I discovered him through a thoughtful piece he wrote in 2011 about my first book in which he noted that "Peter Drucker saw far into the future."

How does he keep an approach/mindset to the future? For him it means "creating rituals that keep us constantly curious, ongoing education that is structured enough to carry weight, but flexible and self-directed to keep motivation high." He also pointed to "the art and habit of visual note-taking," such as the Idea Marathon System from Japan, a creativity development approach developed by Japanese creativity consultant Takeo Higuchi that involves recording ideas daily in a notebook. Reed said, "I swear by [this idea system] and have benefited enormously in accessing both a wellspring of creativity and new levels of attunement in communication."

According to Reed's blog, the steps in the Idea Marathon System, or any note-taking or journal/diary system, involve thinking of at least one new idea per day and immediately writing it down in a notebook kept specifically for that purpose. If you can, illustrate your ideas, à la Leonardo da Vinci, who kept detailed notebooks of his wide-ranging thoughts throughout his life. Keep the ideas alive and growing in your mind by talking about them with other people, both inside and outside the workplace. Finally, put your best ideas into practice. This would seem to be a cyclical activity that works best with constant rejuvenation.

Jason Womack, an author I edited for a 2012 *Leader to Leader* article, "Your Best Just Got Better," has produced some of the best work recently on the role of steady improvement leading to personal transformation. He has written an excellent book on the subject, *Your Best Just Got Better* (2012). Originally a high school teacher in California, he began working as a trainer with one of the best-known people in personal productivity, David Allen, the author of *Getting Things Done*. Eventually he launched his own productivity-based business aimed at helping individuals improve each day.

I asked him to describe the most important things people can do to improve how they work, so they can create their best possible futures. He replied, "How do you define 'productive?'" In a pure, dictionary-sense, it denotes "making something." By applying similar methods to building a physical object or constructing a service, we can step into a creation-like process to move toward the future.

Before he decides to accept a potential client, Womack asks the person to identify, at a personal level, what productivity means. His intention

is to get them to come to this century, as a lot of people are working with a 2000s' (or late 1990s') version of the definition of productive or productivity. This is so significant because the future will be more productive than ever. Or, perhaps more appropriately, we will be more productive than ever in the future. So now is the time, here, in the present, to define what productivity means to you. This is step one for knowledge workers; it must be clear what it is they do, for whom they do it, and how it will be done.

Consider his intriguing definition of knowledge workers, "those of us who think about work, and work on what we think about." Echoing Drucker's importance of the idea of personal contribution, he uses three tactics for knowledge workers to think about the future, starting with knowing their MITs (most important things). Next is understanding when they are at their very best. The final step is imagining what he calls "Ideal Days" for the future.

Womack says that when he first discovered Peter Drucker and *The Effective Executive*, "I too thought that the 'problem' I was trying to solve was that we didn't have enough time." He experimented with Drucker's suggestion to keep a time log of his activities and "found that the more aware of 'time' I am, I change not what time is, how much of it I have, or how long things take. ... Instead, I am much more careful about what I choose to focus on. I think that is the future of productivity."

"Recording time, managing time, consolidating time is the foundation of executive effectiveness."

—*Peter F. Drucker,* The Effective Executive, *1967*

Womack says that his own book has "one intention: to bring to the surface the readers' mindset, how she or he looks at the work through three different areas: how they work, what they think, and where they make [more]."

This is important to the future, because, he says, "to approach a future at a time of such compromised focus and cynicism (we're pulled in many, many different directions, often wondering if what we do even makes a difference), we need to be willing to act 'as-if.' That's what the Ideal Day is all about."

In his words, here is how to determine your Ideal Day: "Take out a piece of paper, and open the calendar to a day out in the future (90 days, 180 days 365 days, to begin) and write a 300- to 400-word overview of how that day turned out to be great. Describe in detail what you did, how it went, who was involved, where you went, and more."

Here is yet another take on time that goes beyond conventional notions of time management: the idea of thinking in long time frames. Tom Butler-Bowdon has written a wonderful series of 50 Classics books; the latest is on philosophy, but he's also written on success, self-help, spirituality, and other topics within the series. In

50 Prosperity Classics, he wrote an insightful chapter on Drucker's *Innovation and Entrepreneurship* (1985).

Butler-Bowdon's *Never Too Late to Be Great: The Power of Thinking Long* (2012) also includes a number of references to Drucker. This book is about making friends, not enemies, with the concept of time. The people he writes about in the book (ranging from Starbucks CEO Howard Schultz to the novelist Lionel Shriver) transformed their lives at least in part by their approach to time.

The book's premise is that significant success, even and especially in middle age and beyond, is possible if you think strategically (and not too impatiently) in long enough time frames. The idea is to work hard and effectively to make your success a reality, including such activities as additional learning, networking, and gaining experience in a field in any possible way.

Butler-Bowdon told me that his approach is to "think long. People are living [longer] now, which means longer productive life spans. We shouldn't worry if our pace of progress isn't as fast as we'd like. We have time. The greatest differentiator in terms of personal success is to have a different sense of time from your peers. If you have a long-term view, you will be more willing to build something that takes decades, instead of going after a short-term result. Remember the saying 'People overestimate what they can achieve in a year but underestimate what they can achieve in a decade.'"

Jesse Lyn Stoner, founder of Seapoint Center, is one of the most impressive people working in the field of leadership development. She has extensive experience as an executive, educator, consultant, coach, and writer. She is highly generative and generous and makes a profound connection with the readers of her blog. She was formerly with the Ken Blanchard Companies and coauthored a best-selling book, *Full-Steam Ahead!* (2011), with Ken Blanchard, a management expert and best-selling author.

In discussing Drucker's concept of a knowledge worker, and what that means in today's world and for the future, Stoner told me:

Until now, knowledge workers have been defined by the amount and type of their formal education. However, the differentiating factor is knowledge, not the system that provides it. One of the transformations brought about by the Internet is the availability of free information and with it the opportunity to learn in nonformal ways. I believe that the current education system will need to reinvent itself and will not be the "bestower" of the real knowledge workers in the future, and, in fact, might not even be now.

She shared her viewpoint that

knowledge does not exist without a network or context to hold it. Individuals cannot hold knowledge and be useful to the system unless they share it. Collaboration is a fundamental underpinning of success. Therefore, knowledge of how to collaborate is as important as having content knowledge. We cannot create the future as individuals, but only through networks of shared meaning. Diversity of thought and perspective is as essential as biodiversity for successful endeavors.

I am impressed with her emphasis on the creation of meaning and its relation to a better future for all. "In my work in helping leaders create a shared vision," she said, "I emphasize that we must dig below our assumptions to find what we most deeply desire. Vision leadership is not about selling a vision to the people. It is about connecting with what they deeply care about and illuminating it consciously. This was the brilliance of Martin Luther King Jr."

Stoner emphasizes an approach that is

driven by curiosity and the willingness to continue discovering. Although I help people create a vision, I also explain that you actually never achieve it. The closer you get to it, the better you understand it, and the larger it becomes. When I discuss characteristics of a compelling vision I explain that a vision should not be about beating the competition. Where do you go after the race is over? It's about being the best you can be. It's not about being number one, because, again, that defines you in terms of your competition instead of where you are going. In fact, the closer you get to your vision, the clearer the magnitude and meaning of the vision become, and it enlarges. There is no such thing as a five-year vision, only a five-year goal. The vision is what answers What's next? after that goal is achieved.

Systematic Abandonment and Kaizen for Individuals: Remove and Improve

Although we will discuss the cycle of systematic abandonment and kaizen for organizations in Chapter 4, these business philosophies can and should be applied to individuals also. Drucker wrote often about systematic (or planned) abandonment. Simply put, it requires that you regularly ask yourself, if you were not already doing a particular activity, knowing what you know now about it, would you start doing it? If the answer is no, think of ways to change the situation. Perhaps you can delegate the activity, or the amount of time it takes can be gradually decreased. Perhaps you can stop doing it altogether.

Drucker believed that systematic abandonment and kaizen worked well together, since, if you have deemed an activity worth keeping, it should be done even better in the future. In his 1992

Harvard Business Review article "The New Society of Organizations," Drucker writes:

> Every artist throughout history has practiced kaizen, or organized, continuous self-improvement. But so far only the Japanese—perhaps because of their Zen tradition—have embodied it in the daily life and work of their business organizations (although not in their singularly change-resistant universities). The aim of kaizen is to improve a product or service so that it becomes a truly different product or service in two or three years' time.

You can practice kaizen, even if you don't call it that, if you are steadily, by trial and error, improving what you do on a daily basis. Small changes can add up to significant improvements.

The idea of using kaizen in a personal sense has become more widespread in recent years. The Japan-based designer Garr Reynolds has described it in this context on the influential "Presentation Zen" blog. Consistent with my premise that creating your future is an approach to life, Reynolds also calls kaizen an approach. "The overriding principle of kaizen is that it is daily, continuous, steady, and it takes the long-term view. Kaizen also requires a commitment and a strong willingness to change," he writes.

Although Reynolds alluded to kaizen for designers, his ideas can be applied to almost any work. He emphasizes that kaizen is long-term and never-ending. You have to become comfortable with the idea that you never really arrive; you are always on the journey. Echoing what we learned from Bruna Martinuzzi in Chapter 1, Reynolds recommends adopting the Zen concept of a beginner's mind. This helps you become more open and receptive to new ideas and concepts because you are not jaded and hobbled by your own experience and preconceptions. Being mindful and aware, looking at things afresh, is a sensible and practical way to approach the future.

Super Successors

Take inspiration from the following examples of people who continue to create their futures, with a track record of succeeding themselves, people that I call Super Successors:

Doug Conant was president and CEO of the Campbell Soup Company for a decade, until his retirement in 2011. In many ways, he has become better known since leaving Campbell.

To coincide with his retirement, he published an excellent, best-selling book, coauthored with Mette Norgaard, *Touch Points: Creating Powerful Leadership Connections in the Smallest of Moments* (2011). (I edited a 2012 article they wrote for *Leader to Leader*, "TouchPoints: The Power of Leading in the Moment.") He became increasingly visible through the book, writing for the *Harvard Business Review* website and developing a new career as a consultant. He also does lots of public speaking and has an engaging website. He has built a large following on Twitter, with his frequent, inspirational, and pithy tweets. He comes across as likeable and approachable, and not as a distant CEO. There is a lot of practical information on his site, and though it is clear that he has moved into the future, he does not disown his past. He includes information about Campbell's on the site, and the book discusses how his leadership approach worked in that company, and how it can be applied and adapted elsewhere.

In July 2013 the Kellogg School of Management at Northwestern University announced that Conant (class of 1976) has founded and will chair a new entity, the Kellogg Executive Leadership Institute.

Edward Tufte has built a fascinating career as the guru of the presentation of graphical and statistical data and information, after 33 years of teaching at Yale and Princeton. He is a master at promoting his ideas, especially through his all-day seminars, "Presenting Data and Information," that he gives nationwide. At 70, he plays a number of roles: an artist/sculptor, author, entrepreneur, teacher, consultant, scientist, and philosopher. He has been self-publishing his large, beautifully produced books, such as *The Visual Display of Quantitative Information* (2001), long before it was the cool thing to do. He is also known to many people for his anti–PowerPoint stance, as explained in a 32-page essay, "The Cognitive Style of PowerPoint: Pitching Out Corrupts Within."

In 2010 President Obama appointed Tufte as a member of the Recovery Independent Advisory Panel. There is a big demand for his work and widespread interest in his activities and thoughts, evident from his considerable media coverage. He is a role model by building on a considerable body of work developed over many years; making his teaching widely available, while being highly entrepreneurial and remaining relevant as he ages. Like Drucker's, his name is synonymous with quality.

Richard Branson has continued to create his own future and remains highly visible as an entrepreneur, executive, adventurer, and blogger/author. In the early 1970s, he started Virgin Records in his native Britain as a mail-order record business that branched out into stores and a record label; later he launched an airline and other disparate endeavors, such as wines, gaming, and Virgin Digital. Branson is a colorful character, and he has been able to leverage his personality and talents in many ways. The Virgin brand became known for having a unique way of looking at the world, of not being afraid of tackling new things, even if it meant entering business niches that already seemed crowded.

Along with the Virgin brand, Branson has his personal brand, which has carried over into writing books, including his autobiography, *Losing My Virginity: How I Survived, Had Fun, and Made a Fortune Doing Business My Way* (2011). He also blogs for *Forbes*, *Entrepreneur*, and other sites. Branson has been able to carry over success into other areas of life, including space tourism with Virgin Galactic. His adventuring contributes to his personal brand, and at 62 he still conveys a youthfulness and daring.

Frances Hesselbein was a longtime collaborator of Peter Drucker's, whom we met in Chapter 2. She is President and CEO of the Frances Hesselbein Leadership Institute (originally Peter F. Drucker Foundation for Nonprofit Management, then the Leader to Leader Institute before adopting its new name in 2012). She has also written three books (the first two have forewords by *Good to Great* author Jim Collins) and edited others.

The institute copublishes the quarterly journal *Leader to Leader*, of which I am the managing editor and Hesselbein is the editor-in-chief. She is a role model to many people worldwide for her abilities in and dedication to leadership and for leading a generative, productive life dedicated to helping others succeed in their own endeavors. She is credited with turning the Girl Scouts into a stronger, more vibrant and inclusive institution during her 14-year tenure as CEO. (She started as a troop leader in Johnstown, Pa., in the 1960s and became CEO in 1976.) Mrs. Hesselbein has the compelling ability to connect on a deep level both in one-on-one conversations, and in speaking to audiences in such a personal way that each person in the audience feels she is speaking directly to them. It's important to remember that she co-founded and built the institute *after* she retired from the Girl Scouts, as she wanted to make a difference in a new arena.

In particular, the institute has remained future-focused, publishing such books as *The Leader of the Future, The Community of the Future,* and others, and producing the Leader of the Future awards annually. You will see the following on the Institute's site: *"Mission: To strengthen and inspire leaders of the social sector and their partners in business and government."* Few people, of any age or in any sector of society, are as mission-driven as Frances Hesselbein.

Daniel Noll and Audrey Scott are a husband-and-wife team of travelers, storytellers, photographers, and knowledge workers with a unique way of creating their shared future. Their travel and work adventures are on constant display on their website, uncorneredmarket.com, and various other social media platforms. They travel the world and document what they see and learn on their site and blog, increasing understanding between people of many different cultures.

Here is Daniel's description of their life in recent years:

After living in Prague, Czech Republic, and working traditional jobs for five years, Audrey and I set off in December 2006 on a creative sabbatical to travel the world for 12 to 18 months. Along the way, we realized it would take longer to discover the world in the way we wanted to. At the same time, we realized there were ways to earn money to extend our journey. For example, we began freelance travel writing, selling our photographs, executing storytelling projects, pitching companies on sponsorship, and selling advertising against the content on Uncornered Market, which continued to grow in popularity.

[As the process evolved,] we used our blog and the experiences in it as a sort of professional portfolio and beachhead of authority connecting consumers and the topics and experiences they were interested in (from travel to personal growth) with companies, organizations, destinations, and contexts that could deliver those types of experiences. Today, we continue to earn money through professional consulting to travel companies and tourism boards, sponsorship, advertising on our website, and speaking. We hope to dedicate more time in the very near future to writing, including a series of books that seek to address the raft of questions we receive from our readers and community.

Danielle Morrill is the CEO and cofounder of Mattermark, a "big data" company formed (with her husband Kevin) in June, 2013. Mattermark helps investors understand the financial progress of more than 100,000 startup companies. Morrill had earlier co-founded and was CEO of

Refer.ly, a social product referral company in Silicon Valley that closed in March 2013. *Forbes* named her as one of the "30 Under 30 for Social/Mobile Technology," in 2011. The tagline on her personal website is "I can see the future, because I live in it today." In 2009 she was the first employee, and director of marketing, for the software company Twilio. Before that she worked for other tech companies and at age 19 began working for Expeditors International, a supply chain logistics company. She's also involved in mentoring and nonprofit work, blogs frequently, and has a large Twitter following.

Morrill provides lots of interesting information about her background and motivations on her website, including how much she learned working at her father's finance consulting company, Reliant Consulting & Research, beginning when she was 12. She's got lots of side activities and continues to study how to write better computer code. She describes her motives for breaking with the past and moving into the future as a company founder/CEO in the blog post "I Don't Do That Job Anymore." Her website connects her with people who want to know more about her wide range of activities and follow her career as it evolves. It's got just enough information without oversharing, including an annotated list of her broad reading. Although from her activities it doesn't look as if she is ever without something to do, she writes that "in my free time I'm working on becoming a better software developer, because I've really learned that when it comes to getting something new started he (she!) who has the code makes the rules."

Conclusion

The metaphor of becoming your own successor will mean different things to different people. No matter how you consider achieving this—from reinventing your work to finding different work—it helps to think of how Drucker achieved and contributed so much to the world over so many years. Keep in mind his personal example of diversifying his output of work, and continuing to be productive into his 90s. Who wouldn't want to remain relevant and influential worldwide as we age?

As you consider the various ideas discussed in this chapter, think of the kind of small but meaningful changes you can initiate right away to help create a better tomorrow. Think about the people and organizations that can help you on this journey, and perhaps how you can help them in return. Who can you contact right away to learn more about furthering your future-focused, long-term thinking? In Chapter 4, we'll look more closely at how to use Drucker's future-related ideas to strengthen your organization, whether it is a business, nonprofit, or other entity.

Chapter Review

We've looked at the different meanings of becoming your own successor and factors within Drucker's life that can guide us through tricky 21st-century landscapes. We have looked at such inner strength tools as mindfulness, the relaxation response, and self-efficacy and considered five minds for the future and ways of thriving at work.

We've explored the suggestions of a variety of thought leaders on ways to work smarter, especially on viewing time as a valuable, rather than scarce, resource. We have also taken a brief look at people who have been successful in creating their futures and becoming their own successors.

Checklist

✓ Think about people you admire, either those you know personally or have learned about. How have they navigated the future? Did they become their own successor?

✓ Check out the websites of some of the people discussed or quoted in this chapter. What parts of their work, and life, resonate with you? Could any become potential role models?

✓ Check online (and/or in books or other printed material) for more information on mindfulness. Look for specific ways it can help you each day to do better work and to better appreciate all areas of your life. Consider taking a class in mindfulness or any mind – body activity. Look for printed and online resources about the relaxation response, and see if you can incorporate it into your life for reduced stress and other benefits.

✓ Look into possibilities for in-person or online learning and teaching opportunities.

✓ Continue adding to your Creating the Future notebook/computer file. This can include material related to the checklist items above.

SHAPE THE FUTURE OF
YOUR ORGANIZATION

4

Many of the insights, ideas, and strategies discussed here are applicable in a variety of settings: not just businesses, but in nonprofit organizations, schools of all types, government agencies, professional associations, and elsewhere.

We will explore a central theme in Peter Drucker's work: that the future requires constant thought and applicable action for an organization to move from its current status to where it should be in the future. Think of this as a continuum; in many ways, you never reach the future, even if you fulfill goals and create things you said you aimed to create.

The idea of the future as a mindset is crucial, because it presents an organized way to consider what actions are needed, starting right now (and ideally yesterday), to create a better tomorrow for your organization—or even to have a tomorrow.

While Drucker believed that the future would remain uncertain and basically unknowable, he saw this as all the more reason to create your own part of the future. You may not have total control over your actions, or the actions of your organization, but you can still accomplish a lot. The world will change anyway, so you must situate yourself to best advantage.

In *Managing in Turbulent Times* (1980), Drucker urged his readers to ask what the world is really like. He also used the term "new realities," which came in handy as a book title in 1989. But the central point is how do you really answer or even consider such stark and visceral questions? Your answers and attitudes determine a lot about how you can shape your business, your career, and your future.

Drucker was the king of tough love for managers. His advice could often be searing, withering, and laser-sharp. A case in point is this passage from the preface of *The Executive in Action* (1996), in which he asserted that "the seemingly most successful business of today is a sham and a failure if it does not create its own and different tomorrow. It must innovate and re-create its products or services but equally the enterprise itself."

For Drucker, then, no matter how successful you are now, merely doing more of it, even doing it better, will not necessarily save your organization in the future. Much of his work was centered on how organizations can evolve to better meet their customers' needs, create new customers and constituents, and serve the wider community and society. A lot of thought and action have to go into deciding what that different tomorrow will entail and how different your enterprise will be.

Yet thinking about the future is not enough. The here-and-now is calling, and it must be answered. In the same book, Drucker states: "Managing the [e]xisting [b]usiness is the first day-to-day task no matter how clear the executive's vision; no matter how brilliantly he or she plans for the future and innovates, today's business has to be managed for results now or there will be no tomorrow." This involves seeking out knowledge, avoiding pitfalls, and determining what are meaningful results.

The Executive in Action is a collection of three of Drucker's most important books: *Managing for Results, Innovation and Entrepreneurship*, and *The Effective Executive*. The first two, in particular, contain important information about navigating the future, and the last focuses on how individuals can further their aims within the organizational context. "Managing the Existing Business" is the focus of *Managing for Results*, whereas "Changing Tomorrow's Business" describes *Innovation and Entrepreneurship*, and "Managing Oneself" is the overriding topic of *The Effective Executive*. While these topics are self-contained within the books, they work together as disciplines. Drucker notes that "business is society's change agent." Other institutions within society conserve or prevent change, he writes, but "business alone is designed to innovate."

This provides us with a handy guide to an approach to the future. Keeping in mind Drucker's thoughts on systematic abandonment and kaizen, you must manage yourself for maximum effectiveness. In both your own work and the work of your organization, you must eliminate activities, products, processes, and the like that have outlived their usefulness or never worked well enough in the first place. You must decide which of these areas should stay in the repertoire and figure out ways to do those things better. Eventually, this will lead to meaningful innovation. But all of this is still not enough. Somehow you must decide what kind of organization you want to have in the future and what your personal role is within that future. What kind of tomorrow do you want to build, and what kind of future do you want to live in and your organization to exist within? How can your organization be a force for good not only within a particular industry or profession, but within society?

In the revised edition of *Management*, Drucker writes, "Management has no choice but to anticipate the future, to attempt to mold it, and to balance short-term and long-range goals. It is not given to mortals to do well at any of these things. But lacking divine guidance, management must make sure that these difficult responsibilities are not overlooked or neglected." Similarly, in the introduction to *Post-Capitalist Society* (1993), he writes, "Yet surely this is a time to make the future—precisely because everything is in flux. This is a time for action."

"It is the individual knowledge worker, who, in large measure, will determine what the organization of the future will look like and what kind of organization of the future will be successful."

—*Peter F. Drucker*, Management, *revised edition, 2008*

Constant, Unrelenting Change through Systematic Abandonment, Kaizen, and More

Constant change is exhilarating but exceedingly difficult. Drucker wrote that people in organizations need stability, even while all this change is happening. This is the responsibility of management, which must not only run the organization well but communicate its values. People can't work well in a chaotic atmosphere. Even as you organize for constant change, you still have to have a vision for why people should work in a setting where change is the norm. Some of this comes about because the outside world is constantly changing, and while things may not necessarily change each day in your own work, you will still be affected by what is happening elsewhere. The nature of that world is constant flux, and constant uncertainty.

In a collection of articles from the Harvard Business Review, *Peter Drucker on the Profession of Management*, Drucker prescribes more tough love, advocating that a business must be balanced between today and tomorrow, that

> it must be organized for the systematic abandonment of whatever is established, customary, familiar, and comfortable, whether that is a product, service, process; a set of skills, human and social relationships; or the organization itself. In short, it must be organized for constant change. The organization's function is to put knowledge to work—on tools, products, and

processes; on the design of work; on knowledge itself. It is in the nature of knowledge that it changes fast and that today's certainties always become tomorrow's absurdities.

This comprises an eternity's worth of activities and could comprise many books on the various areas he covers. These are the ways you get to tomorrow, to live another day. They are not easy and are not meant to be easy.

In the most basic sense, Drucker believed that abandonment must be paired with kaizen, that is, continuous improvement. If you continually improve your products, services, and processes, you often end up with something innovative. In *Managing in Turbulent Times* (1980), Drucker called what later became known as systematic or planned abandonment "corporate weight control." No matter what you call it, you don't want to be on the wrong side of it, because it's one thing to do your own abandoning, but it's another to be part of what's abandoned.

One of the most important points in Drucker's writings is the primacy of change. This represents changes in both individuals and organizations.

When searching for a model for how to deal with change, particularly, how to work with the future in mind, it is helpful to compare what we do with how architects approach their work. They create something that does not yet exist. They build for future use, in many cases for future generations they will not live to see. They build something that must be adaptable to future changes, especially something that may need to be modified or even eliminated. They build something that must be functional and aesthetically pleasing. They must meet exacting standards and ultimately work with teams of other people. They must focus inherently on the new and the different. While aiming for something original and possibly unique, they must be aware of current trends and best practices from other disciplines, such as environmental standards, that will affect or play a role in what they are creating.

Also important to architects' work is that, although changes and adaptations may be made in the future, the completed product is visible and not only has their name attached to it (see Chapter 2 on personal branding), but must stand, insofar as possible, the test of time. Once a building is completed, it is unlikely that major changes can be made. Thus, planning becomes increasingly important.

"The first policy—and the foundation for all the others—is to abandon yesterday."

—*Peter F. Drucker,* Management Challenges for the 21st Century, *1999*

Organizing for Change and More

In *Drucker on Asia* (1997), Drucker discusses the all-enveloping sense of change prevalent at the time that's become only more pronounced since. He writes:

What has changed, and changed profoundly, is our awareness of change. In the past, change was always seen as the anomalous, the exception, perhaps as something that should not be allowed to happen. Societies and groups were organized to prevent change and to maintain stability. We now realize that this does not work. Society and groups have to be organized to take advantage of change.

The idea seems to be to take charge, to make things happen, partly because there will be enough things from the outside that you will have to respond to anyway. Trying new activities, starting new lines of business, and doing things in new, novel ways can all initiate and create change.

Drucker also maintained that change could not be accomplished without sloughing off yesterday by engaging in systematic abandonment. This concept appears in much of Drucker's work. Both systematic abandonment and kaizen should be part of "policies to make the present create the future." Policies in this sense can be thought of as mindsets translated into daily, purposeful actions. Unless you have the mindset that nothing is permanent and that nothing can be taken for granted, you will not be capable of freeing up resources that will yield (or at least have a better chance of yielding) better results in the future.

Being a change leader means focusing more on opportunities than on problems and ensuring that top-notch people are assigned to those opportunities. Drucker equated innovation with making change, making innovation and its various windows of opportunities part of a change policy. I suggest that you organize for constant change by organizing and keeping track of (on paper and/or computer) a variety of things within your life and your organization. By monitoring where you stand in these areas on a regular basis, you are more likely to feel organized for change and for the future. Organize your life around yourself (and your work) in these categories: assumptions, questions, doubts, challenges, changes in process, changes planned, changes stalled, strengths, areas of knowledge and specialization/differentiation, organizational plans, and even your thoughts, mindsets, preconceptions, attitudes, assessments, and feedback, if that is not too nebulous.

You might even list such things as your habits and mental models. How do you see the world? Through what sorts of filters and prejudices? What strategies do you now employ for moving into the future, and how successful are they? How can you construct a new and better reality for yourself? This is a tool for self-organization that helps you see the present as you move into the future. By looking at what you have, you can begin to sense where changes are needed and how you can achieve those changes. What are your fundamentals? What are your basics? Is there room for change?

There are some related questions to organizing for constant change. They are simple, powerful, and basic. Both people and organizations should be able to answer, succinctly but completely, such questions as, What are we doing? How are we doing it? Why are we doing it? What are we going to do? What do we want to do? It is easier to get to abandonment by asking what your organization should stop doing.

You may want to list those people involved or affected by change, including those who are stakeholders and those who should be involved in change efforts.

"One cannot manage change. One can only be ahead of it."

—*Peter F. Drucker,* Management Challenges for the 21st Century, *1999*

Look Out the Window

Baby-boom readers may fondly recall the '60s British Invasion song by the Hollies, "Look Through Any Window," that asks listeners, "What do you see?" Similarly, Drucker's metaphor of the window is a powerful one. In an interview with *Forbes* magazine, he said, "I never predict. I just look out the window and see what's visible—but not yet seen." You have different views and different vantage points, depending on where you look and how you look. You either notice things, or you don't. You and I can look out the window and notice different things. Because we each bring different knowledge, backgrounds, and preconceptions to our viewing, our outlooks and interpretations can differ.

We know that the metaphor of the window goes only so far. Some of things you see (or think you see) may require more information, investigation, or consideration. If all you do is look out the window at one location, especially your location, you miss a lot. However, you can check multiple windows to provide added perspective in your search for the future and to make new innovations. These additional windows may come from travel, intentionally finding new settings within the course of your day (even close to home or work), or even virtual windows from your computer.

Drucker took a holistic approach to the future, considering (1) what you did yesterday, (2) what you do today, and (3) what you envision for tomorrow. The first has such a strong pull and influence on today that it is bound to matter for how you approach tomorrow. Drucker's intense interest in many subjects infused the holistic approach, displaying his wide reading and pleasure in studying and making connections among different disciplines.

What windows into the world do you currently use? How intensively do you look? The metaphor can be as all-inclusive as you want. The viewpoints and experience of your colleagues, friends, and other people can provide windows. Likewise, print and online resources offer different views into the future.

London Business School professor Lynda Gratton, who leads the Future of Work Initiative and was one of the featured speakers at the fifth Global Peter Drucker Forum, in Vienna, was profiled in a *Financial Times* article that stated, "Gratton's varied CV has inspired her distinctive approach. She believes that 'boundary spanning,' as she calls it, is vital. Part-academic, part-consultant, part-businesswoman—she draws on her different experiences and networks to make connections that are not visible to everyone."

This idea of making connections not visible to others aligns well with Drucker's metaphor of the window, as well as with his concept of "living in more than one world." How can we intentionally encourage spanning boundaries in our own life and work? If our corporations and organizations connect with others, the potential for creative synergy is limitless.

"Each window shows some features that can also be seen from the window on either side of it. But the view from the center of each is distinct and different."

—*Peter F. Drucker*, Innovation and Entrepreneurship, *1985*

Innovation and Entrepreneurship

The concepts of similar, interrelated activities can be crucial for an organization's success. For creating the future, individuals in today's world must think and act in innovative ways and have entrepreneurial attitudes, whether or not they consider themselves entrepreneurs. In *Managing for the Future*, Drucker writes: "Systematic innovation requires a willingness to look on change as an opportunity." Again, he encouraged a thought process and an approach with an attitude to openness to surprise, to something different from received wisdom or, as Drucker often put it, what "everybody knows." Frequently, what "everybody" knows is wrong or is ripe for challenging or changing.

Drucker believed that these topics were tied to change that enabled higher, more productive, and better performing yields from resources. But he also believed that all institutions, business or otherwise, needed to engage in these activities, and not just every once in a while or on special occasions, but on a systematic, ongoing basis.

Innovation was seen by Drucker as a practical matter that should not be mysterious. He writes: "Business alone is designed to innovate. No business will long survive, let alone prosper, unless it innovates successfully. And neither innovation nor entrepreneurship [is] 'inspiration', let alone 'flash of genius'. They are disciplines and require concepts, tools, and organized, systematic work." This is consistent with what we have noted in his views on planning, namely, that focused thinking and persistent work and action undergird planning. A similar case can be made for innovation. It is also somewhat similar to effectiveness: a discipline to be learned rather than a sense of genius with which you are born.

Because the concepts of innovation and entrepreneurship have become so familiar and are so studied, we need not delve into them too deeply. There are more books and articles about both disciplines than you will ever have time to read. The key point is to think of them as crucial aspects of discovering and creating a better future for an organization. They embody risk and change and require decisions and action in the present moment in order to bring about the future.

As discussed in Chapter 1, Drucker believed that steadily improving processes, products, and services in the name of kaizen could eventually lead to innovation. Since we know we have to prepare for living in a different world in the future, innovation seems like a reasonable response. In your search for the future that has already happened, and in creating a new future, you can profitably apply the "seven sources for innovative opportunity" that he identified in his classic book *Innovation and Entrepreneurship* (1985): the unexpected (successes/failures and events that happen outside your organization); incongruities; process needs; changes in the structure of an industry or market; demographics; "changes in perception, mood, and meaning"; and "new knowledge, both scientific and nonscientific." He explained that these were listed in order of "reliability and predictability," with new knowledge the least reliable and predictable. These are all open to interpretation and can be difficult to apply.

Drucker also employed the window metaphor in discussing innovation. He wrote that the seven sources "can be likened to seven windows, each on a different side of the same building. Each window shows some features that can also be seen from the window on either side of it. But the view from the center of each is distinct and different."

What process exists within your organization to look for and exploit these opportunities? If there isn't one, how can it be created? Regardless of how much these practices are part of our organizations, we can all look for innovative ways to do our work, and we can all approach our work in an entrepreneurial fashion. If enough of us did this, there would be a great cumulative effect within our workplaces.

Both innovation and entrepreneurship are available to organizations that manage the processes well and that have people collectively willing to think in these ways, on a systematic basis. Success, as we have noted, is not preordained. Some companies can remain innovative, while others may become more innovative.

Also consider Drucker's idea that "the test of an innovation is whether it creates value." He supplied this definition to Frances Hesselbein, for the foreword to the 2002 Drucker Foundation compilation book *Leading for Innovation and Organizing for Results*: "Innovation: change that creates a new dimension of performance."

Innovation is not easy to accomplish. In some ways it is the elusive, holy grail of organizational life. But there are many instructive examples, both in for-profit and nonprofit institutions, especially in the award winners mentioned in Chapter 2. A number of these awards are oriented toward innovation/entrepreneurship.

To give a couple of examples, the Drucker Institute awards the annual Peter F. Drucker Award for Nonprofit Innovation, which was also mentioned in Chapter 1. *The Economist's* Innovation Awards for

2012 included honorees in such categories as bioscience (Napoleone Ferrara of Genentech), process and service innovation (Marc Benioff, chairman and chief executive of Salesforce.com), social and economic innovation (Greg Allgood and Philip Souter of Procter & Gamble); corporate use of innovation (Google), and consumer products (Gary Burrell, chairman emeritus, and Min Kao, chairman and chief executive, of Garmin).

You can find more information and inspiration about successful innovation from the 2013 list compiled by *Fast Company* of "The World's Most Innovative Companies," from the well known (#1: Nike, #2: Amazon) to the less well known (#4: Splunk, a "big data" company) and Fab (#5: Fab, e-commerce). *Forbes* magazine's most recent list of the most innovative companies has Amazon at #2, while #1 is Salesforce.com, also an awardee on *The Economist* list. The global nature of the *Forbes* rankings is evident from such companies as Tencent Holdings (China, #4), Hindustan Unilever (India, #6), Natura Cosmeticos (Brazil, #8), and Bharat Heavy Electricals (#9, India).

Many people would rank companies like Apple and Google at the top of any such list. However, *Fast Company* listed Google at #11 and Apple at #13; *Forbes* had Apple at #5 and Google at #7.

We can also learn a lot from organizations that study and work with business and social entrepreneurs. Social entrepreneurship is the focus of the Skoll Awards for Social Entrepreneurship, given by the Skoll Foundation. The 2013 winners include organizations working for peace and dignity (Independent Diplomat and Crisis Action), education (the Khan Academy and the Citizens Foundation), and health care (BasicNeeds and World Health Partners).

On the business side, there is the Ernst & Young Entrepreneur of the Year Award; the 2012 overall winner was Hamdi Ulukaya, founder, president, and CEO of Chobani Inc., the dairy company known for its Greek-style yogurt. (It was also the #49 most innovative company on the 2012 *Fast Company* list, but it did not make the cut in 2013.)

Very often there is an overlap between innovative companies and entrepreneurial leaders, with the obvious examples of Apple (the late Steve Jobs), Amazon (Jeff Bezos), Google (Sergey Brin and Larry Page), and Facebook (Mark Zuckerberg). Tech-related entrepreneurs include the aforementioned Marc Benioff of Salesforce.com and one of the "super successors" profiled in Chapter 3, Richard Branson of the Virgin Group. The examples don't have to be technology related, however, as seen by Starbucks (Howard Schultz), FedEx (Fred Smith), and Whole Foods (John Mackey). We can't forget Microsoft's Bill Gates, who represents both business and social entrepreneurship, with the Bill and Melinda Gates Foundation. It is obvious that none of these innovative entrepreneurs accomplished their success alone, but instead were able to form companies that could carry out their ideas.

These leaders are all clearly visionaries. They saw potential futures that others did not see, in a variety of fields. They were able to push through difficulties and ignore the naysayers. They had no guarantees that their ideas would be successful, yet they fought on anyway. Few had instant success.

In *The Age of Discontinuity* (1969), Drucker declares that a function of entrepreneurship in the future would be away from one-person-directed enterprises (even if large ones) of the past: "It will rather be the ability to create and direct an organization for the new."

This can have multiple meanings, but it implies a sense of constant change beyond the creation of a new enterprise. And it implies the managerial abilities for self-renewal.

In the same book, he writes, "Yet modern organization must be capable of change. Indeed, it must be capable of initiating change, that is, innovation." Keep in mind that this was long before he wrote *Innovation and Entrepreneurship*. It is a call to keep change high on the list of what is necessary to perpetuate a business or organization.

"Innovating organizations spend neither time nor resources on defending yesterday."

—*Peter F. Drucker,* Management: Tasks,
Responsibilities, Practices, *1974*

Strategic Planning

In the revised edition of *Management,* Drucker writes that "strategic planning is not forecasting." It is an ongoing series of processes. Plans are derived from serious thinking, hard work, and decision making about some bedrock issues about your business or organization. And long-range planning, describing areas with extended futurity and reach of decisions, is built on short-range decisions and actions. No matter what your plans are, Drucker believed that they should become the basis for work assignments and commitments to carry them out.

The most important facet of Drucker's views on planning, without considering time spans or ranges of decisions, is that it is based on thought and research about the current state of your business (understanding your present reality), deciding what your business is going to be and what it should be. He reminds us that the first thing it should be is different from what it is now. It is a mindset based not on forecasting, but on thought, analysis, and imagination. He says that we must ask ourselves, "What do we have to do today to be ready for an uncertain tomorrow?" All of this is predicated on the fact that we know uncertainty awaits, yet we can attempt to do something about it, if we have thought through the issues and decisions clearly enough.

As noted in Chapter 1, Drucker believed that decision making could be conceptualized as a "time machine," with its roots in the present day and the present moment. The decisions made will then play out in a series of time frames. Just as he linked systematic abandonment with kaizen, he tied it to strategic planning. We have to eliminate or at least scale back the no-longer-useful or no-longer-productive in order to have the resources available for the work committed to in strategic planning. He also tied planning with risk. If we have done our strategic planning well, he believed that it allowed organizations to take on greater risk, since we will have a greater understanding of the holistic environment in which the decisions will be carried out. This is a better and more productive use of time than trying to plan to eliminate risk, which he believed was a futile activity. Finally, we need feedback systems that tell us how effective our decisions are.

In *Managing in Turbulent Times,* he notes the need for taking into account how a unique event, something that can't be envisioned, can significantly change the fortunes of a business. This is similar to the "black swan" effect we have come to associate with the author Nassim Nicholas Taleb. Leaders and managers obviously have to preserve the best of their organization's values, talents, and efforts, but simultaneously they must ensure that there will be a meaningful future, far into the future. In the same book, Drucker writes that "today's executives are also charged with the responsibility for making the future of the business, with lead times that are becoming ever longer and in some areas range beyond ten years."

He follows this up by saying, "Performance in management, therefore, means in large measure doing a good job of preparing today's business for the future."

Regarding strategic planning, in the revised edition of *Management,* he writes, "What do we have to do today to deserve the future?" We can infer from this that no organization is guaranteed to live forever, or even into the short term. Again, his tough love approach says that organizations must earn the right to live another day. It is a powerful call for responsibility and courage. And it issues a challenge, which is so characteristic of Drucker's work, to both prove an organization's worth and then prove that it has the capacity to compete in the inevitable new landscape that tomorrow will bring.

As he noted in *Managing in a Time of Great Change* (1995), you can use the techniques of looking for the future that has already happened as a way of planning in an uncertain world. The question becomes, in his words, "What has already happened that will create the future?" Taking this a step further, organizations can determine how they can create their own future, within this larger societal future. Part of that involves knowing those things at which you excel. He notes the similarities of his own construct of "strengths analysis" to Gary Hamel and C. K. Prahalad's "core competencies," made famous in their book *Competing for the Future* (1994).

Long-range planning could be mere wishful thinking if you have not seriously thought about how decisions will be carried out, in what time frame and by whom, and whether or not your organization has the talent to make those decisions effective.

"Planning is not an event."

—*Peter F. Drucker,* The Five Most Important Questions You Will Ever Ask about Your Organization, *2008*

The Future of Work Takes Work

As we can see from the featured quote in this section, Drucker believed that creating the future required a daily, purposeful, roll-up-your-sleeves approach. It is similar to the notion that innovation doesn't require genius but lots of hard, thoughtful work, and also that we can't count on superheroes to run our organizations; ordinary people must become capable of doing extraordinary things.

We have to ask ourselves, on an organizational level, similar questions to what we asked when considering the future as individuals. What kind of world do we want to live in and create? What kind of world do we want others to live in? What will it take to get there? The future will not be handed to us. Even the mightiest companies can stumble.

Drucker's ideas about what makes a responsible approach to the future, applicable for people and for organizations, revolve around responsibility, duty, service, practicality, and challenge. As decisions are made, work is assigned and duties are drawn up to cause the future to happen. Plans can be changed or tweaked as necessary along the way, because as the world changes, plans may need to be changed accordingly. New technology can become available. Competitors may spring up who did not exist yesterday. Laws may change.

We want the future to be better than the past and better than our current situation. But we know that it will not just happen, and if we continue to let time slip away, we will have less ability to influence the future. Work on the future demands thought and deliberation to decide what kind of future we really want, even if we can't know all the details beforehand. It demands that we become and remain forward thinking. We must build in a discovery process and take ownership of a sense of discovery. The ideas we discussed in Chapter 2 about finding the future are particularly relevant here. There are countless ways the future can happen, but it is up to us to put our imprint on the future so that it will be different than it would have been otherwise.

Everyone in the organization needs the forward-focused mindset. Almost any decision should be made with the future in mind. Is this decision best for the long term as well as the short term? What are the possible unforeseen implications? A systematic approach is needed. an approach where we remain open-minded and observant about possible directions for the future and trust in our own talents to make it happen, even if that means bringing in new people and ideas. We become, in a sense, explorers charting new territory. Part of this approach is factoring the effects for future generations, not just people affected in the present.

"To make the future happen requires work rather than genius."

—*Peter F. Drucker,* Managing for Results, *1964*

Competitive Intelligence

In Drucker's world, companies need to be forever future- and forward-focused. The focused searching we discussed in Chapter 2 can be a perfect component in developing a competitive intelligence (CI) strategy for your organization. There is not one overall accepted definition for this term. However, it involves gathering and monitoring, on an ongoing basis, information about not only current and potential competitors, but about the news, research, regulatory and related landscapes in which a business or other organization operates, or is considering entering in the future. This research can be done formally or informally, by individuals or groups, and either with or without specialized software or consultants. For the purposes of this chapter, we'll look at it as a do-it-yourself activity. However, I have asked three of the top people in the field—Arik Johnson, founder and chairman of Aurora WDC, an intelligence research, systems, and training advisory firm, and managing director of the Center for Organizational Reconnaissance; Craig Fleisher, chief learning officer and director of professional development of Aurora WDC; and Chris Hote, CEO/USA of Digimind Inc., an intelligence software company—for their brief appraisals of why

CI can be crucial for companies as they work on creating their futures. Their replies will also give you a better idea of what CI entails.

Hote calls CI a "discipline" that should ideally report directly to executive management and include

- Field intelligence
- Monitoring and analysis of competitors (in such areas as mergers and acquisitions, hiring, product launches, investment, and technologies)
- Monitoring and analysis of consumers or customers

We've discussed the importance of understanding the present reality and how the future unfolds by the decisions and actions we take in the present moment. We want those decisions to be as well informed as possible. This is where CI comes in. It aims to help us identify the landscape in which we operate (or in which we would like to operate), as well as the major players and why we should know what they are doing. This could mean current competitors or potential ones. CI can inform our strategy and also help us to leapfrog the competition by understanding what they do and how we can do it better. Different parts of an organization can use CI to help them improve their work, understand more about what they are doing and why, and identify potential profitable markets and niches.

This sort of investigative work would have been much more laborious and hit-or-miss years ago. Today, with so many sources of information readily available online, it is much more powerful. Still, it's not easy, and it takes a lot of effort. It must be iterative and occur daily. Your goal is to discover important information that can be crucial to the current and future operation of your enterprise.

If building the future, and alleviating some of the anxiety about it, means strategically using and managing the best information possible, we have to figure out the best ways to do it. You can investigate the websites of these and other CI companies, including the webinars and other information tools offered by these companies.

As Arik Johnson points out, opportunities can be missed by focusing too exclusively on what goes on within a company, as important as that can be. Drucker, as we know, argued that we have to look beyond our four walls and be open and receptive to information from a variety of sources. Part of that can entail, as Craig Fleisher says, field research. Drucker advised executives to get out of the office and meet customers, noncustomers, and potential customers in their own habitats.

Another reason that CI is so important is that, by its nature, it is forward-focused and is all about turning data into information into knowledge. This fits right into Drucker's dictum that information must be organized to challenge a company's strategy. In other words, not only do you have to organize the information for optimal use, you need it to be strong enough to both inform and back up your decisions about strategy. CI makes it possible to reduce risk by understanding as much about the current and potential business environments as possible. As Fleisher says,

Competitive intelligence is, by design and tasking, a process that helps executives in organizations to envision a more desirable future. Unlike many better known organizational functions that rely on reorganizing and tabulating prior performance data, CI activities and practices are designed to help decision makers look ahead, and many also help managers to "peer around corners." Indeed, in the absence of well-performing CI activities and processes, organizations will arguably be ill-prepared to engage in a more desirable future of their own influence and making, and instead be buffeted and driven by the winds that other organizations and stakeholders generate.

To learn more about Fleisher's insights on how organizations can move into the future, read the second edition of *Analysis Without Paralysis: 12 Tools to Make Better Strategic Decisions* (2012), the book he coauthored with Babette Bensoussan.

Hote finds within Drucker's work on marketing "a particular focus on customer satisfaction, customer intimacy, and customer retention." An important question then becomes, according to Hote, "How can organizations maintain a sustainable competitive edge from better knowing, anticipating, and meeting their clients' needs?" This is where CI can be valuable. Its role has been growing quickly in recent years, according to Hote,

> fueled by the substantial and constantly increasing amount of information available on the Internet. Beyond newspapers, press releases, corporate announcements, and corporate websites, the Internet now contains numerous databases (patents, clinical trials), public information (regulatory bodies), and user-generated content (blogs, Twitter, Facebook, and so on) that can be exploited to better anticipate market trends, competitor tactics, and consumer demands.

As Drucker himself wrote in *Managing in a Time of Great Change* about the importance of finding and using information for an organization, "Most of what the enterprise needs to know about the environment is available only from outside sources—from all kinds of data banks and data services, from journals in many languages, from trade associations, from government publications, from World Bank reports, from scientific papers, or from specialized studies."

Finding this information at the time he wrote this could be laborious and difficult, not to mention expensive. Much of it is now easier to find; however, because there is so much, information overload is a much greater problem. Yes, there is a lot of free information available on the Internet, but there is also a considerable amount that is available only for a fee, including the services of CI companies.

As Johnson notes,

> Strategic, market, and competitive intelligence overcomes traditionally internally focused leadership by placing strategy as the product, rather than the process, for defining and achieving success. The bygone era when strategy and marketing were separate disciplines has enabled an intense focus on generating new demand and quantifying customer value by solving customer problems, often before customers even knew they had them. An effective intelligence apparatus taps into this curiosity and knowledge of the outside world and redirects a formerly nearsighted, outside-in focus externally so organizations can learn faster than their peers. This process of transforming mysteries into heuristics and then further into algorithms accelerating the flow and evolution of knowledge in the organization is rapidly becoming the definition of leadership in the 21st century.

For those in large corporations, a source of information is the organization's own library. Many corporate librarians have developed specialties within the CI field and work with the databases of CI companies. Many corporate librarians are members of The Special Libraries Association/SLA, the group Drucker delivered the keynote address for at its annual conference in 2002. The SLA has a Competitive Intelligence Division. You can learn more about the division's members and activities at its website, http://ci.sla.org/.

To learn more about independent CI specialists, you can contact the nonprofit membership organization Strategic and Competitive Intelligence Professionals (SCIP, www.scip.org).

Drucker wrote often about trained perception and the ability to see patterns—crucial attributes of people engaged in CI. Looking at the same data or information, what can you perceive that no one else can? How can you communicate its importance? Why should everyone else on your team be aware of it? What are the strategic possibilities?

CI professionals deal with many different parts of a company, so they are likely to have a better overview of a company's needs and possibilities. These professionals also leverage sources such as social media, which have become an increasingly important factor in all aspects of corporate operations.

As we discussed in Chapter 2, there is more good information out there than you will ever have a chance to read, digest, and understand. This is only going to become more pronounced in the future, especially with so much user-generated content in so many formats. You must accept that you'll never be able to keep up with all that already exists, much less what continues to arrive in your in-box, Twitter feeds, Facebook status updates, LinkedIn updates, and so on. If done correctly, CI can keep you from drowning in these data.

Former Drucker School adjunct professor Joseph Lee, who teaches at both Chuo University in Tokyo and Pepperdine University in California, says, "In this new world of almost unlimited information, it will not be the one who knows the most who wins, but the one who knows what's important and what's not. The ability to have challenging discussions will be at the core of someone who wishes to succeed."

"Information is data endowed with relevance and purpose."

—*Peter F. Drucker,* The Ecological Vision, *1993*

Using Appreciative Inquiry to Discover the Future

You can help devise the future of your organization through practices that are not solitary, that instead involve your colleagues and other stakeholders. For example, there is appreciative inquiry (AI), a method that emphasizes what an organization does well rather than focusing on what it does poorly.

Too many organizational exercises these days dwell on what has gone wrong, will go wrong, is going wrong, and not on what has gone well, which often seems to be taken for granted by company executives. AI (not to be confused with CI) builds on the positive, which fits in with Drucker's idea of building on an organization's strengths and minimizing its weaknesses. As part of a suite of techniques for building a corporate future on an ongoing basis, AI can be quite powerful. People inherently want to do good work, after all, and often take pleasure in and gain power from hearing about islands of excellence that are already within a company.

Because AI is inherently question-based, it lines up perfectly with Drucker's own question-oriented approach. Drucker often used questions in his books and when consulting; we'll discuss his use of questions, including in this book *The Five Most Important Questions You Will Ever Ask about Your Organization,* in Chapter 5.

AI has been associated with positive psychology, a relatively new concept that has become prominent in recent years, especially through the efforts of its pioneer, Martin E. P. Seligman, a professor at the University of Pennsylvania, where he leads the Positive Psychology Center. He is also the author of the books *Authentic Happiness* (2002), *Learned Optimism* (2006), and *Flourish* (2011). In essence, positive psychology is the study of what is right with people, rather than what's wrong. According to the center's website,

Understanding positive emotion entails the study of content-
ment with the past, happiness in the present, and hope for
the future. Understanding positive individual traits consists
of the study of the strengths and virtues, such as the capacity
for love and work, courage, compassion, resilience, creativity,
curiosity, integrity, self-knowledge, moderation, self-control,
and wisdom.

Jeremy Hunter and Mihaly Csikszentmihalyi, whom we discussed
earlier in this book, are allied with this field.

Although companies often conduct AI exercises using consultants and professional trainers, you can follow the do-it-yourself
approach that we emphasize in this chapter. Basically, you want to
determine what works. If something is working well in one part of an
organization, chances are that it can be adapted and used elsewhere.
Perhaps it can even be improved upon.

One of the leading proponents of AI is David Cooperrider of
Case Western Reserve University, who has been a visiting professor
at the Drucker School and in 2010 was named as the Peter F. Drucker
Distinguished Fellow by the school. His efforts focus on creating positive change, change that innovates and creates new possibilities for
both organizations and the people they serve—their employees and
other stakeholders, the community, and society as a whole.

AI speaks to uncovering the potential that is already within an
organization, somewhat similar to what knowledge management the-
oretically aims to do to leverage the knowledge that already resides
in an organization. You may also want to couple your AI practice,
which focuses on the inside, with your practice of CI, which focuses
on the outside.

A big part of AI is the idea of co-creation, that you do not have
to do everything on your own, that you don't have to reinvent the
wheel. If there are visionaries within your company who are not

known beyond their divisions, it is possible that they will become better known through AI.

AI speaks to the sense of curiosity that was so much a hallmark of Drucker's work and that can be cultivated by any of us. This process of questioning sharpens and focuses our minds. Besides, wouldn't we all rather be positive than negative? Doesn't it create a better form of energy and renewal for the future?

What You Can Learn from the High Line

Visionaries can be found in any setting, of course, not just in the business world. Joshua David and Robert Hammond qualify in this category, as the driving forces behind the development of the High Line elevated public park in New York City. The project had its beginnings in 1999, when David and Hammond, who had no experience in urban planning or design, got the idea to save a portion of elevated rail line on Manhattan's West Side that was in danger of being demolished and convert the rail bed into a planted green area. Through their efforts and the efforts of other community residents, in association with the city, the elevated structure was preserved, and an attractive public space was created, complete with lawns and gardens, walking paths, viewing areas, and vendor setups.

Besides being an inspiring place to relax and people watch, the new space is environmentally friendly and has had a huge, positive force on the development of buildings and businesses in the Chelsea neighborhood. Since its opening in 2011, it has become a magnet not just for New Yorkers, but for people from around the world. That same year, David and Hammond published a book about their journey, *High Line: The Inside Story of New York City's Park in the Sky*.

Hammond stepped down in 2013 as the executive director of the Friends of the High Line, the group he and David formed with other community members to preserve, promote, and run the park. David has remained as chief development officer. The key point here is that, despite their inexperience, Hammond and David had vision and passion, as well as the fortitude and smarts to make a difficult venture happen and to make it an ongoing success. The project certainly was risky, with no guarantees, but by making the High Line such an attractive and inviting, not to mention unusual, space, they opened up all kinds of possibilities for others.

Though the park is completely free, businesses have arisen near it, and value has been created that did not exist before. There is a real sense of change involved, because the neighborhood (along with related development efforts) changed for the better; indeed, it has been transformed. It should be noted that this change was happening before the creation of the High Line, but it has accelerated since. It took a lot of "present moment" work to make it happen, especially considering that the park opened 12 years after Hammond and David originated the idea, after meeting at a community board hearing.

New York's High Line is a great example of social entrepreneurship, and it has inspired similar efforts in other cities worldwide. It is also an example of what is possible when you show that something seen as difficult really can be done. People can learn from your example and put their own distinctive twists on it. Presumably, High Line–type parks that rise in other cities will have different features that relate more to their own surroundings. Just as the work of companies has an effect, consider how changes in civic space can have amazing ripple effects and make a difference in the lives of many different people, far into the future. This is especially true when what could have been wasted space is turned into something truly meaningful.

What ideas can you and your organization create that will inspire others? What can you prove is really possible? How can you exercise the art of possibility? It is a powerful idea that someone (or a group of people) can look at what already exists and imagine a totally different future from how others see it, then make it go beyond an idea to see that it actually happens.

What You Can Learn from Landmark College

Another inspiring story of innovation comes from Landmark College, in Putney, Vermont, which pioneered college-level studies for students with dyslexia and other learning disabilities.

In recent years, it has become clear that many more people than previously thought have dyslexia and related learning disabilities, such as attention deficit hyperactivity disorder and autism spectrum disorders. People can be highly talented, intelligent, and creative, yet have trouble learning in traditional classrooms because of the way their brains process information. Highly accomplished people, such as discount brokerage founder Charles Schwab, Cisco CEO John Chambers, and Virgin's Richard Branson are dyslexic. They are also models of creativity, innovation, and entrepreneurship. Yet if so many people are afflicted by these disorders, and we are only recently becoming aware of their extent, how can we educate students in the best way so they reach their full potential? This is where schools like Landmark come in. Its tagline is "the college of choice for students who learn differently."

Founded in 1985, the school employs, among other things, universal designs for learning, which, according to the National Center on Universal Design for Learning, "provides a blueprint for creating instructional goals, methods, materials, and assessments that work for everyone—not a single, one-size-fits-all solution but rather flexible approaches that can be customized and adjusted for individual needs." It borrows from architectural principles of accessibility and access. I discovered that the term was started by Ronald L. Mace, who died in 1998 at the age of 56. He was described as a visionary in articulating these principles and was the founder of the Center for Universal Design (separate from the educational organization noted above). Again, we have a visionary who saw things in different ways, perceived different and useful configurations that others did not, and managed to do something about it.

Having a school of higher learning that is focused on only this type of student is not only innovative, but fairly revolutionary. And note this Drucker-like comment on its website: "We embrace students' strengths." This is an obvious case where weaknesses are minimized, and strengths are built upon. I don't know if Drucker was aware of this school, but I believe he would have approved of the finding and exploiting of a particular niche, a need in society, and creativity and innovation in learning. Plus, his love of learning and realization that different people learn in different ways are at the core of what this school represents. Landmark wants to be a leader and a trailblazer, and its administrators, along with the faculty and students, are certainly creating change, not just managing it.

As we learn more about learning disabilities, will there be other schools that are focused on how to best educate these people? Could this be the beginning of a significant new trend in education? And can it have a ripple effect for corporate education? Presumably, there are many people with learning disabilities who are working for companies that offer educational opportunities. How can these people be accommodated?

On the Landmark website, the president of the school, Peter A. Eden, underscores a number of Drucker-like items in outlining the school's commitment to making a meaningful difference in the world:

Our commitment to continued change, growth, and new ideas ensures that students who learn differently will always have access to the programs and services they need for academic success and career advancement. We do all of this together. In doing so, we change the way the world thinks about education, and the way our students think about themselves as leaders."

Conclusion

Your business is in the present, as well as the future. The question should be not only how can not only you get there, but how can your organization and the people in your organization get there with your help, guidance, and vision?

Tomorrow starts today. In fact, it started this morning, even before you awoke. That's literally the case with different countries in different time zones, but it is also a metaphorical reality. We can't waste time that could be spent building and developing our future, for our business and for ourselves and our colleagues.

People and organizations both must be organized for constant change, which can be uncomfortable and upsetting. Drucker believed that amid the constant change, the management of an organization should also provide a sense of stability. In Chapter 5, we will look at ways individuals can build their future through activities beyond their main workplace, and in cultivating the mindsets needed to be most successful.

Chapter Review

We've examined Peter Drucker's main topics for advancing your organization into the future, especially systematic abandonment, kaizen, organizing for change, innovation and entrepreneurship, and strategic planning.

We've also looked at some areas not specifically Drucker-related that can be valuable ways of surfacing the future: competitive intelligence and appreciative inquiry. And we've looked at two highly innovative (nonbusiness) initiatives from which businesses and other organizations can learn: the High Line park in New York City and Landmark College in Vermont.

Checklist

✓ As an exercise in systematic abandonment, list several products, services, and/or processes offered within your organization. If they were not currently offered, would you want to start them? If not, how will you proceed to eliminate them, or scale them back?

✓ Check out the websites of competitive intelligence companies Aurora WDC and Digimind to learn more about CI. If your organization is not already employing it, consider starting at least a rudimentary program on your own.

✓ Pick at least three Drucker quotes in this section that are most meaningful to you, and see how accurately they describe your organization.

✓ What one technique or topic in this chapter was most intriguing to you? What can you do within the next 24 hours to learn more about it, including finding out if any of your professional colleagues are knowledgeable in this area?

✓ Continue adding to your Creating the Future notebook/computer file.

BUILD YOUR FUTURE BEYOND YOUR CURRENT WORKPLACE

5

As I discussed in *Living in More Than One World: How Peter Drucker's Wisdom Can Inspire and Transform Your Life* (2009), an important part of Drucker's worldview was the sense that, as important as work is, it can't be the only thing in one's life, or the sole source of satisfaction and self-worth.

We will now look, in a broad sense, at ways we can build a future that go beyond the work we do now, in our current workplace. We will look at how what we do now, in the present moment, can lead to a better tomorrow for us as individuals, as a part of families, and in the wider community and society. We will explore Robert Kegan's writings on adult development and how we can better approach our futures by cultivating a sense of self-authorship and perhaps even self-transcendence.

The focus is on who you are as a person now and who you can become. We must factor in that the development process never ends, except, of course, with our death. Yet the fact of our inevitable death, at a time that remains mysterious and hidden from us, concentrates our mind on making the most of the time we have now and whatever time remains for us. We must remain forward-focused until the end, and that means forward-thinking until the end.

In some sense this is a continuation of the "inner tools" segment of Chapter 3. Chapter 5 emphasizes cultivating our inner lives; understanding ourselves in all aspects (work and otherwise) that help us see more clearly who we are, what we believe, and what we value; and deciding how we can take that into creating a better future. This represents a search for meaning as we move through our transitions in life, no matter what age we are now. How can we make sense of who we are now and where we are going? This is a search for personal growth, and it can be done in as many areas of life as we want to address.

Our first stop, though, is looking at an aspect of Drucker's life and thought that has been examined more in recent years: the role of the spiritual in our lives.

The Spiritual and Transcendent World of Peter Drucker

The roots of Drucker's views on the spiritual and the religious, and how those views played out in his teaching and writing about management, have been analyzed in great detail in the years since his death. Readers who would like to know more about Drucker's religious (specifically Christian) beliefs will find much to consider in two scholarly articles: "The Practical Wisdom of Peter Drucker: Roots in the Christian Tradition" by Timo Meynhardt of the Center for Leadership and Values in Society, University of St. Gallen, Switzerland, published in 2010 in the *Journal of Management Development*; and "Peter Drucker's Leap *to* Faith" by Susana Fernandez of the H. Wayne Huizenga School of Business and Entrepreneurship, Nova Southeastern University, Davie, Florida, and Florida Atlantic University, Boca Raton, Florida, published in 2009 in the *Journal of Management History*.

Another in-depth source is Joseph A. Maciariello and Karen E. Linkletter's book *Drucker's Lost Art of Management: Peter Drucker's Timeless Vision for Building Effective Organizations* (2011). Maciariello was a longtime colleague and friend of Drucker's at the Drucker School and was his coauthor for three of Drucker's books that were released posthumously: the revised edition of *Management* (2008), *The Effective*

Executive in Action (2006), and *The Daily Drucker* (2004). Linkletter was the first archivist at the Drucker Institute and is a historian who teaches American studies at California State University at Fullerton.

The explications in their book and the two articles cited are deeper and more involved than the scope of *Create Your Future the Peter Drucker Way*. My emphasis on this particular part of Drucker's life and work is on the need to reach our highest levels of potential, to become our best self, and to improve our own lives and the lives of others. This is a part of spirituality, and it resonates throughout Drucker's work, even if it was not specifically labeled by him as such.

One fascinating element of Peter Drucker's work is the undercurrent of becoming a better person, of making your life truly count, which certainly contains a spiritual element. He was privately religious but did not talk much in public about his faith or religion. Yet the articles mentioned above and others that have focused on the religious background of his work remain fascinating to me. I am not writing from a religious standpoint, and I am not a theologian. I am approaching this topic as a spiritual issue: how we can grow and develop as human beings, how we can serve others and see beyond ourselves and our private concerns to the wider world. It also speaks to serving something—a cause, belief, organization greater than ourselves, especially something that will live on beyond our lifetime.

The religious references in Drucker's work are not hard to find. He said that he learned more about theology as a management consultant than when he taught religion (which was early in his teaching career). He set one of his two novels, *The Temptation to Do Good* (1984), in a fictional Catholic university.

During a trip to Tokyo in 2012, one of the most moving experiences for me was a visit to a Shinto shrine. Even though I know next to nothing about this faith, just being in the presence of believers, in the open air and inside the shrine, was inspirational. It also provided a sense of peace. The idea that anyone can access that same sense at any time during the day is comforting. I myself draw strength from a number of religions, without necessarily believing in their complete creeds.

I can't give you a scholarly explication of Drucker's 1949 essay "The Unfashionable Kierkegaard," a personal examination of the work of the Danish philosopher and theologian Søren Kierkegaard (1813–1855). The essay originally appeared in the *Sewanee Review* and has been anthologized in at least two books. It is a statement of faith that he described as one of the best things he ever wrote. (For a more in-depth look at this article, see particularly the Maciariello–Linkletter book referenced previously.) I can only give you a visceral reaction to it, as well as my sense of why it is important. Just the fact that he attempted an article like that is significant. It is also significant that we accept it as a crucial part of his canon, along with the works on management and the rest. (And consider the coincidence that Kierkegaard died on November 11, 1855, and Drucker died on November 11, 2005.)

When "The Unfashionable Kierkegaard" was anthologized in *The Ecological Vision* (1993), Drucker gave, in a short introductory essay, a kind of personal spiritual statement that was deep and revealing. He writes: "My work has been totally in society. But I knew at once, in those far-back days of 1928, that my life would not and could not be totally in society, that it would have to have an existential dimension that transcends society. Still, my work has been totally in society—except for this essay on Kierkegaard."

This would not be his first and last foray into a discussion of faith. In *Landmarks of Tomorrow* (1959), yet another future-oriented work, he writes: "Society needs a return to spiritual values—not to offset the material but to make it fully productive." That book also references the concept of I and Thou, as articulated by the great philosopher Martin Buber, with whom Drucker studied while in college in Germany. Drucker also claimed that this return to spiritual values was needed because mankind needed compassion. He wrote that humanity "needs the deep experience that Thou and I are one, which all higher religions share."

Drucker emphasized, like a preacher, that the individual must return to spiritual values,

> for he can survive in the present human situation only by reaf-firming that man is not just a biological and physiological being but also a spiritual being, that is, creature, and existing for the purposes of his Creator and subject to Him. Only thus can the individual know that the threat of instant physical annihilation of the species does not invalidate his own existence, its meaning, and its responsibility.

This sentiment appears to foreshadow some of the ideas in Rick Warren's multimillion-selling book *The Purpose-Driven Life* (2002). There are also the familiar themes of meaning and a sense of responsibility. The nature of the threats to existence may be somewhat different today than in 1959, but we are always threatened as a species and always will be. It seems to me that this call for a combination of faith and responsibility is a powerful one.

The concept of legacy was important to Drucker. In *Managing the Non-Profit Organization* (1990), he writes: "I'm always asking that question: What do you want to be remembered for? It is a question that induces you to renew yourself, because it pushes you to see yourself as a different person—the person you can become."

Drucker challenges us to live with the end in mind—not only the end of our own lives (not always easy to think about), but also what will be left in the hearts and minds of people who live on beyond us. In Drucker's case, and I suspect for many of us, this will include the effects of our lives on people we don't know personally or who have not yet been born.

It is a powerful statement and call to action for the future, in that Drucker says it engenders a sense of renewal and a state of becoming. If you are not satisfied with where things are now, do something about it. If the idea of a legacy spurs you to action, that's fine, but I think it also means accepting the need for renewal and becoming a different person. This relates to what we discussed for individuals in Chapter 3 and for companies and organizations in Chapter 4. The future will be different from the present. What role will you play in defining that difference?

The idea that Drucker thought seriously about renewal and meaning, along with and probably related to his work on management, organizations, and society, reveals his interest in an existence beyond, though not excluding, material achievement.

In a compelling article, "The Romantic Generation," written for *Harper's* in May 1966, Drucker wrote about the baby boomers then in college. Think back to that era of change and unrest. One part of the article (later included in the 1971 collection *Men, Ideas and Politics*) discusses where young people of that generation would fit in "a society of big organizations." He writes, "In such a society of big organizations, the need becomes more urgent for new answers to the old questions, Who Am I? What am I? What should I be?"

Because Drucker published so many essays in a variety of publications, he would sometimes use or adapt some of the material in subsequent books. This is evident in parts of the following passage, which were later used in 1969's *The Age of Discontinuity*, but the wording was changed and expanded. Drucker said that individuals should think beyond a career to "a demand that the individual take responsibility for society and its institutions." Then the wording of the above questions changes slightly: "The society of organizations forces the individual to ask of himself: 'Who am I?' 'What do I want to be?' 'What do I want to put into life and what do I want to get out of it?'"

These questions are fairly similar to those he believed organizations should ask about themselves. In *The Five Most Important Questions You Will Ever Ask about Your Organization* (2008), they are, What is our mission?, Who is our customer?, What does the customer value?, What are our results?, and, What is our plan?

The significance of these questions is the future dimension: What should I be? To answer that, you have to do something about the future through your actions, thoughts, and decisions in the present.

Drucker was an early commentator on large pastoral churches, what have come to be known as megachurches. He worked early on with Rick Warren of Saddleback Church in Lake Forest, California, and Bill Hybels of Willow Creek Community Church in South Barrington, Illinois. An interview with Warren, by Rich Karlgaard of *Forbes*, appears in Drucker and Maciariello's *The Effective Executive in Action*. Drucker had a long-standing friendship and working relationship with Bob Buford, introduced in Chapter 3, who led him into the megachurch milieu. He also wrote the forewords to two of Buford's spiritually oriented books, 1994's *Halftime* and 2001's *Stuck in Halftime*.

Besides Buford, Drucker attracted other high-level leaders with strong spiritual backgrounds. In particular are Max De Pree, the retired CEO of the innovative company Herman Miller (which is a major backer of the Drucker Institute), and C. William Pollard, the retired chairman and CEO of ServiceMaster. Buford and De Pree were both interviewed in *Managing the Non-Profit Organization*. At the time, De Pree was on the board of the Fuller Theological Seminary in Pasadena. Although he is retired now, his legacy has been extended through the Max De Pree Center for Leadership. He has written several books, including the classic *Leadership Is an Art* (2004).

Pollard wrote a spiritually oriented book about ServiceMaster, *The Soul of the Firm* (1996), which contains a considerable amount of Drucker-related material. It also features this Drucker endorsement on the cover: "Bill Pollard tells us in *The Soul of the Firm* how to manage the large service business and give its employees dignity, productivity and meaningful work." Besides being clients, Buford, De Pree, and Pollard had deep personal friendships with Drucker.

To complete the circle, Maciariello wrote a short but revealing book tying a number of these themes together, *Work and Human Nature: Leadership and Management Practices at ServiceMaster and the Drucker Tradition* (2002), which was published by the De Pree Leadership Center, as it was then known.

My sense is that people who are particularly spiritual or religious are drawn to Drucker. Yes, there is religious imagery within Drucker's work, but it goes beyond that. Drucker's work speaks to a high sense of self-development and personal transformation, coupled with morality and personal integrity.

As seen in his classic book *The Effective Executive,* there is also the sense that our society requires executives who have developed into effective people who can organize the tasks needed for everyone to survive and thrive. Drucker gently downplayed the personal development angle, particularly in these sentences from the book's conclusion: "There is little danger that anyone will compare this essay on training oneself to be an effective executive with, say, Kierkegaard's *Training in Christianity*. But only because the goal is so modest can we hope at all to achieve it; that is, to have the large number of effective executives modern society and its organizations need."

The question becomes, how can we take Drucker's work in these areas and apply them for our own purposes, especially as they relate to the future? Could it be that specific areas of religion and spirituality help us get a stronger sense of what the future may hold, or that their sense of optimism helps lead us to a bright future?

Obviously, people who already have strong and specific religious faith can draw from their belief system on how they go about making the future. They might feel that a certain amount of the future is predetermined in some way.

In the book *Post-Capitalist Society* (1993), Drucker discussed the "existential goals" of redemption, self-renewal, spiritual growth, goodness, and virtue and tied them to individual responsibility. These goals can also serve as a beacon for our own development. The main point is that different people will have different ways of attaining those existential goals, perhaps through religion, partly or completely, or it may not. If it is through religion, it will necessarily be different religions for different people, and different ways of approaching and working through these goals. It could be through some spiritual sense that has the feeling of religion, yet is fundamentally separate from it.

Drucker's list of goals is congruent with areas that help us develop as fulfilled individuals. It can help us answer the question, what should I be? It also ties into Drucker's legacy questions, about pushing yourself to become a different person.

"'The Unfashionable Kierkegaard' was thus written as an affirmation of the existential, the spiritual, the *individual* dimension of the Creature. It was written to assert that society is not enough—not even for society. It was written to affirm hope."

—*Peter F. Drucker,* The Ecological Vision, *1993*

Spiritual Reading

Another way to access the spiritual and the sense of the sacred is through reading. The most obvious example is through daily or less frequent reading of the Bible and other religious texts.

In a 2004 interview with Drucker for *USA Today* as he was turning 95, one year before his death, I asked him what he was rereading. He replied, "I always read a little in the Bible—mostly either the Psalms or the Epistles of St. Paul. Just now I have begun rereading the Epistles and find them very exciting and full of insights earlier readings didn't reveal."

I have to feel that Drucker's reading and rereading of the Bible helped provide clues to the future, both for himself and for society. I think it is important for all of us, no matter how advanced we are in years, to look for these clues, and to continue to create our future, even if that future may be measured only in days, not months or years.

There are, of course, numerous religious and spiritual books, plus specialized journals, magazines, and websites. As with other types of reading, there is never enough time to get through all the good material. Everyone will have their own favorites and new discoveries. One book I eagerly await each year is the latest in *The Best Spiritual Writing* series, edited by Philip Zaleski. (The first edition was published in 1998.) These essays and poems that had been previously published in a variety of publications are invariably thought-provoking and eloquently written. They are windows into a variety of spiritual practices, inquiries, and even doubts and uncertainties. The books invariably introduce me to writers I had not known about who enlarge my sense of the spiritual.

I highly recommend the 2005 book, *50 Spiritual Classics,* part of the *50 Classics* series by Tom Butler-Bowdon, whom we met in Chapter 3. Following the format of the series, he provides concise and well-written chapters on books of "inner discovery, enlightenment and purpose," from a variety of spiritual and religious traditions, placing them in historical context and with brief quotations. There is an emphasis on what we can learn from the central messages of these books to lead to a deeper, more spiritual, improved life. You can decide if you want to explore these writers more thoroughly, but *50 Spiritual Classics* gets to the core of each book, so you gain a good level of understanding about a wide variety of authors and their work, including St. Augustine (*Confessions*), Carl Gustav Jung (*Memories, Dreams, Reflections*), Shunryu Suzuki (*Zen Mind, Beginner's Mind*), Eckhart Tolle (*The Power of Now: A Guide to Spiritual Enlightenment*), and Warren (*The Purpose-Driven Life*).

Earlier publications in this series contain related books. For instance, in 2003's *50 Self-Help Classics,* we find the Bible, the Bhagavad Gita, and the Dhammapada (the Buddha's teachings), as well as writings by the Dalai Lama and Lao Tzu's Tao Te Ching.

To learn more about high-level spiritual books, Frederic and Mary Ann Brussat compile the Best Spiritual Books of the Year, categorized by topic, from the more than 300 reviewed each year on the Spirituality & Practice website.

Reading about spiritual and religious topics can be a wonderful source of inspiration. I believe that inspiration is one of the major things we seek, when we access the spiritual and the religious.

People will have different conceptions of what it means to be spiritual or religious. I include some fairly brief sections below that can help us understand more about the spiritual quest and how it relates to our future. While they are not specifically Drucker-related, I believe that they mesh well with his values and what I understand about his quest for spiritual understanding. I hope that in reading them, and contemplating their meaning and their relation to your own life, now and in the future, they can help you focus more on what really matters, what is most important to you. I believe that reaching toward the often elusive sense of the spiritual can help us organize and better use the unknown amount of time we have on earth.

"Faith is the belief that in God the impossible is possible, that in Him time and eternity are one, that both life and death are meaningful."

—Peter F. Drucker, "The Unfashionable Kierkegaard" (1949),
in The Ecological Vision, 1993

The Inspirational Huston Smith

If we are going to draw inspiration from someone in the world of religion and spirituality, a terrific author to read is Huston Smith, an American religious studies scholar and author who grew up in China, as the son of missionaries. He is now in his early 90s and mainly retired, though several Smith-related books have been published in recent years, including 2009's *Tales of Wonder: Adventures Chasing the Divine, an Autobiography.*

Smith is known for his multimillion-selling book *The World's Religions*, originally published in 1958 as *The Religions of Man*, later published in a 50th anniversary edition in 2009. He was also the subject of a fascinating, five-part PBS show in 1996, *The Wisdom of Faith*, a series of interviews conducted by Bill Moyers. In addition, Smith had his own educational series in the early years of public broadcasting.

The importance of Smith's work on comparative religion was further brought home to me recently by reading Warren Bennis's January 13, 2013, blog post "Does Religion Belong in the B-School Curriculum?" on the *Bloomberg Businessweek* site. Bennis is the dean of leadership writers, known for such classics as *On Becoming a Leader*. He was also a longtime friend of Peter Drucker's who wrote about him perceptively.

Bennis makes the case that business schools should offer a course "on the impact of religion on everyday life," in order for MBA students to fully comprehend the "global mind." (The latter brings to mind Drucker's comment to me about the importance of the global worldview; see Chapter 3.)

I've long considered Smith to be a Drucker-like figure. Both remained relevant and productive deep into old age, were renowned authors, professors, and wisdom figures, and were considered to be at the top of their fields. Smith includes an anecdote about Drucker in the 2001 book *Why Religion Matters: The Fate of the Human Spirit in an Age of Disbelief,* winner of the Wilbur Award for best book on religion.

I also find commonalities in the writing styles of Smith and Drucker: both are clear, direct, and compelling. This style allowed them to effectively convey complex ideas to wide, diverse reader-ships in readily accessible terms. Smith shares with Drucker a deep curiosity about the world and about how things relate to each other. Smith's academic career was wide-ranging, including teaching stints at Massachusetts Institute of Technology, Washington University in St. Louis, Syracuse University, and the University of California at Berkeley.

Smith and Drucker share an interest in the Far East. Smith enlightened Western audiences about Eastern religions, and Drucker, of course, is known for introducing readers in the West to Japanese management, as well as to Japanese art and related knowledge about the Japanese people. One of the chapters in *The World's Religions* is on Confucianism. In a further tie to Drucker, Edward J. Romar of the University of Massachusetts, Boston, wrote an extensive article in 2004 for the *Journal of Business Ethics*, "Managerial Harmony: The Confucian Ethics of Peter F. Drucker."

In addition, there are commonalities in their personal lives. Drucker was married for 68 years, and Smith has been married for 65.

Smith, like Drucker, writes for both the committed student and the interested layperson. He is an ordained Methodist minister, yet practices a number of religions. He emphasizes the practices, teachings, wisdom, and personal benefits of the major religions in his books and deemphasizes the institutional side of religion. His ability to increase human understanding about a sprawling, difficult subject is admirable. I also believe that, as we discussed in Chapter 3, Smith built a long-term career by doing something that helped other people, had a worldwide audience, and was based on an ever-growing, high-quality body of work. He had multiple venues for that work: on television, in the classroom, and in his many books and the many interviews he granted for a variety of publications.

Wouldn't many of us like, in our 90s, to look back on a long, productive life that benefited others in tangible ways? The only way for that to happen is to integrate the ongoing work on a daily basis. None of us know if we will have a Drucker/Smith-like life span, but we can work toward it, figuring that it could happen, and that we would like to reach old age with few regrets.

Just as Drucker's clear and direct writing makes us want to learn more about management, organizations, and individual self-development, so do similar qualities in Smith make us want to learn more about the world's religions: their messages, teachings, what they have in common, and why they can be an important component of a person's life now, thousands of years in the past, and, presumably, thousands of years into the future.

What We Can Learn from a Study of College Students and Spirituality

The college years are a time of discovering what is important to us personally and of continuing to chart a life into the future. In our world today, this quest continues for many of us beyond college, even if the nature of the quest changes. That is one reason why I believe it is relevant to look for clues to our continued adult development in a major study, begun in 2003, of spirituality conducted by Alexander W. Astin, emeritus professor, and his colleagues at UCLA. The study, titled "A National Study of Spirituality in Higher Education: Students' Search for Meaning and Purpose," surveyed more than 14,000 students at 136 colleges and universities nationwide.

While Astin may not be as well known as Drucker or Huston Smith, he is still a tremendously influential figure, probably comparable to Stanford's Albert Bandura, whom we met in Chapter 3 and will meet again in this chapter. Astin, with his wife, Helen S. Astin, and Jennifer A. Lindholm, all of the Higher Education Research Institute (HERI) at UCLA (where he is the founding director), conducted the study and later published *Cultivating the Spirit: How College Can Enhance Students' Inner Lives* (2011). (The study, incidentally, was funded by the John Templeton Foundation, the organization behind the Templeton Prize, which we discussed in Chapter 2.)

Reading about this study made me think back to the essay Drucker did for *Harper's* referenced previously and the questions he said needed to be raised by college students of that era, beginning with, who am I? I don't think the need has changed much in the ensuing years for students (and everyone else) to be asking these questions.

The inner life is highly important in how we determine our futures or try to influence the future for other people. The study covers such crucial areas as meaning, purpose, discovery, values, and beliefs. This gets at the whole notion of being, of why we exist. Explorations into these areas can help us discover answers for an overarching question: What's the point of what we are trying to do with our lives in the limited time we have on earth?

The components of the study can serve as a concise guide to the religious/spiritual quests of any person, college student or not. According to the report's website (http://spirituality.ucla.edu/findings/), the study looked at five spiritual and five religious qualities. The two sets of qualities reveal different categories, but certainly with some crossover. The spiritual qualities are *equanimity* (how well one responds to life's circumstances and challenges, including feelings of centeredness and life direction), *spiritual quest* (active search for meaning and purpose and the answers to the big questions of life; meditation and self-reflection can be particularly important here), *ethic of caring* (how much the individual cares about other people, and the world at large, including issues of suffering and social justice), *charitable involvement* (not only giving money to charitable causes, but also helping friends in times of need and being involved in community service), and *ecumenical worldview* (a global worldview somewhat similar to what Drucker advocated; this involves understanding of and tolerance for others, especially those with different religious backgrounds, and the ability to see interconnections among all people and cultures).

The religious qualities are *religious commitment* (how strong a role do spiritual/religious beliefs play in life?), *religious engagement* (including praying and reading religious/sacred texts and attending religious services; this is the more active complement to the "internal" construct of commitment), *religious/social conservatism* (in the language of the report, this "reflects the student's degree of opposition to such things as abortion, casual sex, and atheism, as well as an inclination to proselytize and to see God as a father-figure"), *religious skepticism* (nonreligious views about the origins of the universe, not believing in an afterlife, and a future-related belief that "science will be able to explain everything"), and *religious struggle* (disillusionment; questioning or feeling distant from one's religious beliefs and religious upbringing; feeling distant from God).

When considered together, these categories strike me as being relevant for organizing the feelings on these major topics for people of almost any adult age group. If we consider them from a future perspective, they take on added significance. You could look on any of these areas as potential goals for the future, or as a partial guide to activities that you think could add more meaning, purpose, and significance to life. Because some of these activities are solitary and some can be thought of as more group-oriented, they may be a way of adding new and different people to your life. These qualities also reflect the future perspective in the sense of improving the future lives of other people.

This speaks to Drucker's notion of seeing yourself as the person you can become and grow into. Any of us, whether college students or not, might want to look at these categories and see if we agree or disagree with them, if any could be added or dropped, and to compare where we stand now in each category with where we would like to be in the near and long-term future.

"Man, if he owns a spiritual nature in addition to his physical, psychological and social being, can never be entirely controlled by the 'knowledge' of totalitarianism."

—*Peter F. Drucker,* Landmarks of Tomorrow, *1959*

Spiritual Modeling

You may want to become more spiritual but have difficulty finding ways that work for you and that deepen your own sense of what that means. In this case, you may find "spiritual modeling" to be a useful tool.

In 2003 the *International Journal for the Psychology of Religion* published an invited essay, "Spiritual Modeling: A Key to Spiritual and Religious Growth?" It was written by Doug Oman of the School of Public Health, University of California, Berkeley, and

Carl E. Thoresen of the School of Education Departments of Psychology and Psychiatry, Stanford University.

Commentary included Albert Bandura's "On the Psychosocial Impact and Mechanisms of Spiritual Modeling," along with an authors' response by Oman and Thoresen, "The Many Frontiers of Spiritual Modeling." We discussed Bandura, the renowned Stanford University emeritus psychology professor, in Chapter 3 in the context of his powerful theory of self-efficacy.

The central idea of spiritual modeling is that people can learn effectively by modeling the messages, teachings, and, in some cases, behaviors of chosen spiritual exemplars. The obvious examples include figures such as Jesus, the Buddha, and Muhammad. As the authors note, in these cases the models will not be physically present, so "devotees are urged to remember the words and deeds of these persons and to seek to live by the same guiding spirit." They also note that the exemplar does not necessarily need to be the founder or most well-known figure associated with a religion, but could be a family member, someone from the community, or a mystic. This means close observation, a skill and attribute I associate with Drucker. They use the term *observational spiritual learning*. These spiritually related skills, they contend, can lend themselves to such admirable traits as "wise living and effective self-regulation." Because religion and spirituality are so heavily based on wisdom traditions, this makes a lot of sense. It also makes sense for building a better future by becoming a better, wiser human being. Besides Bandura, the article by Oman and Thoresen references Huston Smith, whom we discussed earlier in this chapter.

Oman and Thoresen emphasize that while many religious traditions have various aspects in common, spiritual growth does not necessarily have to be about "sets of doctrines and behavioral codes." They also point out that spiritual searching can be about areas such as identity, belongingness, meaning, health, and wellness. Trying to adhere to the teachings and requirements of a particular religion may mean actively seeking to become more truthful, charitable, calm, humble, and generous and less grasping. These attributes call for "high-level skills such as comprehensive self-regulation and accurate judgments of one's own or others' motivations." Within what the authors refer to as "observational learning" (part of Bandura's social learning/social cognitive theory), they contend that people can learn more of these skills and behaviors than they could through trial and error or even by being directly instructed. They note that Bandura said that the processes governing this observational function were attention, retention, reproduction, and motivation.

In this context, attention can relate to the focused attention of mindfulness, which we discussed in Chapter 3. Retention can include repetition, as in prayers, songs, hymns, and stories. In a table, the authors provide spiritual modeling examples, including such models as people with whom one would have direct contact, such as "fellow congregants," and a "spiritual director," as well as "scriptural figures" and models within such frameworks as meditation, reading, and "verbal rituals." They also note that aspects of spiritual modeling can work in nonspiritual/religious contexts, such as in 12-step programs.

As we seek to deepen our own spiritual and/or religious lives, we can try to think more explicitly about where we learn our behaviors in these realms, such as observing others that we trust and admire and would like to emulate, as well as what we read. What is highly pertinent for our discussion is how this reading and observation can improve our lives in the future.

In the related commentary article, "On the Psychosocial Impact and Mechanisms of Spiritual Modeling," Bandura notes the applicability of self-efficacy to spiritual modeling. "Seeing people in similar circumstances succeed by perseverant effort in the face of difficulties raises observers' beliefs in their personal and collective efficacy to change their lives for the better and to shape the social future," he writes.

Bandura also discusses symbolization in how people understand and manage their lives. He writes: "The capacity for forethought enables people to transcend the dictates of their immediate environment and to construct and regulate the present to fit a desired future." In this "future-time perspective," we think about goals, our motivations, and how we see our future playing out, in regulating our life in the present. We also think about the possible consequences of what we plan to do. "Through exercise of forethought," he writes, "people motivate themselves and guide their actions anticipatorily. When projected over a long time course on matters of value, a forethoughtful perspective provides direction, coherence, and meaning to one's life." These thoughts and actions can be learned and strengthened through modeling, which is the tie to Oman and Thoresen's writing on spiritual modeling.

Leading a meaningful, spiritual life is not easy. If we accept that enhancing and deepening our spirituality is a worthwhile goal, then investigating avenues of spiritual modeling makes sense. Drucker must have been thinking along those lines in his reading of the Bible, the works by Buber and Kierkegaard and probably many other sources, given the wide nature of his reading. What models will you follow, and how seriously and strategically will you follow them?

"The inner knowledge of one's own unification in God—what St. Paul called hope and we call saintliness—only a few can attain. But every man is capable of attaining faith. For every man knows despair."

—Peter F. Drucker, "The Unfashionable Kierkegaard" (1949),
in The Ecological Vision, 1993

Healing and Our Sense of the Spiritual

Drucker wrote often about nursing, and the role of nurses within the wider setting of a hospital. He conveyed the importance of allowing nurses to do the main work they were trained to do, instead of spending so much time filling out paperwork. I'm not aware that Drucker knew anything about Jean Watson and her organization, the Watson Caring Science Institute and International Caring Consortium, but I find some interesting commonalities in what both find important in life.

Watson is a distinguished professor emerita and dean emerita, University of Colorado, Denver, a fellow of the American Academy of Nursing, and the author of a number of books and articles. She has gone beyond nursing to showing the vast possible dimensions, including the spiritual and mysterious, of the healing arts. Since empathy and compassion have been shown to be so important in medicine, it stands to reason that Watson's caring science will only become more important in the future. Just as Drucker had an outsized influence in management, Watson has been highly influential in nursing, both in hospitals and in schools of nursing.

Watson's "10 caritas processes," outlined on the institute's website (http://watsoncaringscience.org), while perhaps in language that we would not associate with Drucker, still outline a powerful, compelling vision of what healing can entail. The vision is also future oriented and forward thinking because the whole idea of healing is to transform the present, to move from something unsatisfactory to something better ' and improved. A major theme of *Create Your Future the Peter Drucker Way* is improving life; this is an instance where life is being improved for others. The connections are striking. For instance, #10 (Be open to mystery, including the spiritual; allow miracles to enter) speaks to the idea of tolerating uncertainty and ambiguity; #7 (Share teaching and learning) is right out of the Drucker playbook; #6 (Use creative caring decision making) speaks to creating something that did not exist before; #3 (Be sensitive to oneself and others; includes the idea of cultivating spirituality); and #2 (Instill faith and hope) speaks to the idea that in order to create our best futures, we need to cultivate a sense of hope, of positive aspiration. These practices/principles would seem to have wide applicability for our personal and professional interactions with others in daily life.

The idea of caring science, and human caring, is bound to have an influence beyond the field of nursing in the future, as we become more aware of fields such as self-care and the benefits of linking compassion and spirituality with health. With health care becoming such a crucial yet contentious field, it's obvious that new, creative, and holistic models will be needed.

Adult Development

As important as the spiritual realm can be, it is worthwhile to look into theories about how our minds and thought processes develop as adults. One particular avenue of interest is the mental complexity model developed by the Harvard theorist Robert Kegan. It has implications inside and outside the workplace, for how you move toward your future and how you think about ways to get there. It also has implications for related areas such as volunteering, or nonprofit or pro bono work, that you may engage in now or in the future. This self-reflection will help us stop and consider where we are now in our mental development and where we can go. In the words of Stanford University psychologist Carol Dweck, we know that it is best to take a "growth mindset," rather than a fixed one. If we believe we can learn and grow as we continue through adulthood, the levels described by Kegan and Lisa Laskow Lahey in *Immunity to Change* (2009) as "plateaus of mental complexity" can be crucial. All of us cope with increased complexity and ambiguity, so any help we can get to understand why we do things is helpful. It also helps us to understand our present reality, so we can best decide on courses of action for the future.

How we think about the future, and what we believe is possible for us, will inevitably be influenced by the filters we employ now in day-to-day life. Kegan and Lahey delineate three plateaus. It could be that at various times we will exhibit ways of thinking using all three, though in most cases we act on only the first two levels.

The **socialized mind** is the first level of complexity. This type of mind is a team player and a follower, and tends to be more reliant on others for setting direction and deciding what is important. None of these are particularly bad qualities, but they are probably limiting for leadership opportunities or creativity and original thinking.

The **self-authoring mind** is the next level in complexity. With this mind, individuals are much more in charge of writing their own life story and developing their own belief systems separate from others in their environment. This requires a "step back" from the environment to decide what is best based on a person's own codes, judgments, and values. This is the level at which most leaders think, and it lends itself to those who are problem solvers and independent of mind. Kegan and Lahey point out that such decisiveness can be a problem if the person is wrong, or if things change in the environment, causing his or her judgments and plans to be flawed.

The **self-transforming mind** is the highest level of complexity and is rare. It represents an advanced capacity for learning and change and an orientation to finding problems more than solving them. It is also the highest level of independence and, crucially, requires the ability to hold contradictions in one's mind. This too requires a step back, yet in this case it is a step back to observe and determine one's own limits and beliefs. The self-transforming mind can look at multiple points of view and contradictions in a clear, holistic way. Kegan and Lahey make a crucial point about how this relates to the future.

The self-transforming mind "is aware that it lives in time and that the world is in motion, and what might have made sense today may not make as much sense tomorrow."

This framework helps us to think about our own ways of doing things, of how much we take into account the views of others or the wide number of viewpoints in the outside world. It speaks to the changing nature of the world and how we can keep that in mind as we continually review our habits, and how those habits affect everything we do. It also provides a way to view our relationship with change: least comfortable with the socialized mind and most comfortable when we are self-transforming. But don't feel bad if you are not in the latter category. Kegan and Lahey note that it is still rare, is something to aspire to, and may only be reached by a few people.

In 2012 I worked with Jennifer Garvey Berger, who had studied with Kegan at Harvard, on an article for *Leader to Leader*, "Cultivating Wisdom." A principal at the New Zealand consulting firm Cultivating Leadership, she discusses some of these same adult development themes in the article and in her insightful book, *Changing on the Job: Developing Leaders for a Complex World* (2012). I asked her about the aspects of her work that are future-focused. "In my own work," she said,

> the adult development ideas help us think about how much of the future different people can grasp—and how abstract their sense of the possibilities might be. We all know that earlier in our lives, we are more present-oriented, and we think rather narrowly about the impact of events (often just those things that affect us or those to whom we are particularly close). A rich and nuanced view of the future—as well as the sense that we can work to create (or author) our own future rather than having more of an "audience" relationship to the future—comes later in our developmental journey.

A Holistic Look beyond Your Current Workplace

Drucker often wrote about the need to have genuine interests beyond your main work. He cited such reasons as keeping yourself alive, young, and growing and developing leadership experience, gaining intellectual stimulation, and as a way of guarding against the inevitable disappointments that come with any job. When his 834-page book *Management: Tasks, Responsibilities, Practices* was published in 1974, he wrote a short piece for the *New York Times,* "Memo to Managers: Find Outside Pleasure." It contained some similar outside-of-the-job themes as in his 1952 article in *Fortune,* "How to Be an Employee," which was reprinted in his *People and Performance: The Best of Peter Drucker on Management* (1977). In it he introduced a new term, the "counterculture of amateurs." (One of the many highlights of the 1952 article was an emphasis on sharpening one's ability to communicate in writing and speaking. He urged his readers to take courses in writing poetry and short stories, to better learn economy of language, organization of thought, and how to understand the nuances of communicating meaning via the written word.)

As he describes it, this counterculture of amateurs would run in a different time frame from the main culture of large organizations, the kind being managed by so many of Drucker's readers. This was something that went beyond a hobby, where you have a fairly serious interest and a stake in doing it well. Ideally, you become more than a dilettante. (He uses an example of a highway engineer who plays viola in an amateur string quartet.)

It is difficult to tell if this counterculture ever really appeared, but it is a good way to start thinking of the wide range of activities involved beyond our career. Some of them can be work-related, just not related to your job. You also might consider ways to move into other jobs or other lines of work that would take you out of your present workplace. For all the reasons listed here, meaningful outside activities are helpful as we continue to create our futures. The following list is certainly incomplete, but it gives you an idea of the world beyond the four walls of your job:

- Family activities of all types
- Volunteering
- Mentoring
- Spiritual/religious activities
- Taking classes (not necessarily the types listed in Chapter 3, although they are also valid, but also classes offered in your community, places of worship, etc.)
- Playing and/or teaching a musical instrument or learning how to play one
- Music appreciation
- Clubs
- Book groups
- Dancing
- Professional associations (yes, this is work-related, but outside the confines of the job)
- Playing sports
- Exercise/mind–body activities
- Involvement in civic groups
- Involvement in alumni associations
- Gardening and anything nature-related
- Part-time jobs

While all of these activities can offer meaning and a sense of growth in the present, they can all be thought of as future-oriented as well. They can help you formulate goals for the future, or serve as pilot tests for things you'd like to do more seriously in the future.

"But perhaps more important, the society of institutions needs something the nineteenth century spurned: the genuine amateur who is capable of accomplishment and performance in one area outside, beyond and independent of his job."

—Peter F. Drucker, "Memo to Managers: Find Outside Pleasure," New York Times, May 5, 1974

Meaningful Retirement

In some ways, Peter Drucker never retired. Although he considerably slowed down, he did both consulting work and teaching well into his 90s. He also published books and articles until nearly the time of his death at 95, in 2005.

The baby-boomer generation is now rapidly moving into retirement or thinking about what retirement might entail. The financial downturn in recent years has meant that many people who would like to retire will have to delay or redefine retirement. Others may have had retirement plans moved up because of the unavailability of jobs in their current field or at the level they now hold.

As health care improves and people take better care of themselves, they will be living longer. This could mean that many will not be interested in a traditional, leisure-oriented retirement. For some, the answer can be volunteering, assuming they have the financial resources. For others, it may mean part-time work. One organization, Encore.org (formerly known as Civic Ventures), has been at the forefront of considering "Encore" as a new stage of life. The leader of the organization, Marc Freedman, has published such books as *Encore: Finding Work That Matters in the Second Half of Life* (2007, which includes some material about Drucker) and *The Big Shift* (2011).

This organization is a great source of information about how to navigate meaningful retirement, no matter what you choose to call it. Each year, it awards the Purpose Prize (which we noted in Chapter 2). This is partially funded by the John Templeton Foundation (also see the Templeton Prize in Chapter 2). The Purpose Prize honors five people age 60 and over each year, at $100,000 each, for their work and entrepreneurship in social innovation. That's because a goal of Encore.org is to encourage individuals to use their talent and ingenuity to help communities and society, especially by trying to solve long-standing problems. The 2012 winners include Bhagwati Agrawal, executive director of Sustainable Innovations Inc., who is bringing safe drinking water to his native India; Susan Burton, founder and executive director of A New Way of Life Reentry Project, who is helping female parolees rebuild their lives after prison; and Judy Cockerton; founder and executive director of Treehouse Foundation, who is working to improve the lives of children in foster care. The latter was the winner of the Purpose Prize for intergenerational innovation, which was sponsored by AARP, another institution that can be a major source of ideas and information on the Encore stage of life.

No matter your age or stage of life, you should think about the second half of life and how to redefine it for your future. In addition to these organizations, your community may have a variety of institutions that can help you formulate a strategy for making the most of the most important time you have: the present and the way you use the time in the present to plan for a better tomorrow.

Creating the Future for Others

As we consider how to create our own futures, perhaps it is a good idea to stop and consider how we can directly affect the future of other people, especially future generations of leaders and significant contributors in our professions or other areas of interest.

We've discussed education a lot in this book. One area that can have a major impact on the lives of others is either contributing to scholarships (perhaps at your alma mater) or, if you are in a position to do so, creating scholarships that can help develop the next generation of professionals and leaders. For instance, each year the online information company ProQuest (mentioned in Chapter 2), under its Graduate Education Program, gives the Roger K. Summit Scholarship. It honors Dr. Roger K. Summit, the founder of Dialog, a pioneering online business, which is part of ProQuest. The scholarship, which is now in its 20th year, is worth $5,000 and is open to library and information science graduate students worldwide.

Another interesting example is the Watson Fellowship, in which $25,000 each is granted yearly by the Thomas J. Watson Foundation to a number of graduating college seniors for independent study and worldwide travel. The foundation honors the work of Thomas J. Watson Sr., the late founder of IBM and someone whom Peter Drucker wrote about extensively.

As a side benefit, these scholarships also provide good publicity for the organizations that award them. But the larger issue is that they help fund the work and education of promising people who can move their professions into a better future not just for themselves, but for everyone else.

Conclusion

A major part of our discussion in this chapter has been about spirituality and religion. Were you surprised to learn of Drucker's involvement in these areas? Did learning this, or learning more about this, change your perception of him at all? If so, how?

This might be a good time to consider to what extent you would like to change or augment the work you do in your current workplace. Of the activities listed above, which ones are you already doing, and which ones seem doable in the short run? What are more long-range projects? Which ones are of no interest at all to you? Considering these is a valuable exercise.

In the final section, we wrap up our journey to the future, although, as we've seen, the journey is best viewed as never-ending.

Chapter Review

In this chapter, we have looked at the spiritual and transcendent aspects of Drucker's work, and what you can learn from them. We have considered other aspects of spirituality and religion, such as what you can learn from a major study about the spiritual lives of college students. We have also looked at how people can better develop their spiritual lives by "spiritual modeling."

We've looked at the spiritual/religious writings and life of Huston Smith for inspiration as well as information, as well as the caring science, related to healing and its spiritual aspects, of Dr. Jean Watson.

Because this book is about mindsets, we've examined the mental complexity model developed by the Harvard theorist Robert Kegan; including his explanation of three levels of increasing complexity: the socialized mind, the self-authoring mind, and the self-transforming mind.

Finally, we've glimpsed the wide range of possibilities for life beyond your career, including Drucker's "counterculture of amateurs."

Checklist

✓ If the spiritual/religious material in this chapter resonates with you, make a list of any involvement you currently have in this realm and what you'd like to add in the future. What people and/or organizations are involved, or could be involved?

✓ What educational opportunities (large and small) in this chapter resonate with you? What is your plan to learn more about how you can take advantage of these opportunities?

✓ What are your answers to the questions Drucker proposed: Who am I? What am I? What should I be? What do I want to be? What do I want to put into life, and what do I want to get out of it? What do I want to be remembered for?

✓ Are you involved in any of the beyond-the-main-workplace areas listed at the end of the chapter? If there are some that you would like to add, what is your next step to learn more so you can take action? What other activities would make sense for you to add to this list?

✓ Continue adding to your Creating the Future notebook/computer file.

CONCLUSION: YOUR FUTURE BEGINS TODAY

One of the goals of this book is to help you organize your thoughts, plans, and actions about the future. I have tried to make the concept of creating the future as concrete as possible.

Although the book has come to an end, ideally you will continue to reread sections of it for inspiration and as circumstances change in your life inside and outside the workplace.

We have examined how the life and work of Peter Drucker can be an indispensable guide to the future. In particular, we saw that he cultivated a mindset for thinking about and acting on this unknown territory. His longevity, having lived until almost age 96, is at least in part a testament to the success of his approach.

Your Creating the Future notebook/computer file can be a valuable tool to you now and far into the future. If you have not been adding to it as much as you had planned to, now is an excellent time to restart. If you are keeping your eyes and ears open, and keeping an open mind, there will never be a shortage of material to include.

This notebook is valuable because it records not just what you learn from other people and discover online and in print, but what you yourself think. What are your hopes and dreams for the future? How have they changed while reading this book? How do you expect they will change over time?

Periodically, reread what you have written to see the progress you have made or to identify areas you would like to change or improve. I have encouraged you to add to the file in the checklist of activities at the end of each chapter. But now that you are finished reading, you will not have those prompts, unless you pick up the book again from time to time. That's why it is a great idea to add to your notebook/file as many days of the week as you can, even if you jot down only a thought or two each time.

Throughout the book, I have encouraged you to imagine the kind of world you'd like in the future and what it would take to get there. I've suggested that you broaden this to thinking about the world for not just yourself, but for others, starting with those closest to you, but extending beyond to the wider community and society.

In this book, we have explored ways that both individuals and organizations (businesses and otherwise) can move forward into a better future.

To briefly recap some of the main areas of the book, in Chapter 1 we looked at various elements of the future prominent in Drucker's work and what role those elements might play in your own future. In Chapter 2 we looked at ways to discover "the future that has already happened," through both face-to-face and online activities. Chapter 3 covered individual success factors for the future, what I call "becoming your own successor." Chapter 4 examined organizational success for the future, including how we can employ tactics such as competitive intelligence to learn as much about the current and future landscape as possible. Finally, in Chapter 5 we examined both the spiritual and religious aspects of your life beyond your main workplace, as well as the role of adult development in defining your future.

Because so many sources have been listed in this book, Drucker-related and others, I have included a web resources section for you to return to as much as necessary, which I hope is often.

I would love to hear from you about your own plans for the future, especially how I could further help to aid you on your journey. Please email me through my website, www.brucerosenstein.com. In addition, I will include considerable information about how to create the future on the site. I hope your future is full of health, success and prosperity, and that this book will have played a significant role.

A SELECTED READER'S GUIDE TO DRUCKER'S WRITINGS ON THE FUTURE

Many of Peter Drucker's books included references to the future. In this brief section, we take a look at some of the more prominent ones. It is meant as a guide to your further reading, to help you gain the deepest understanding of his work on this important topic.

All of Drucker's books are worth reading and rereading. His collected works are in many ways awe-inspiring. They contain a lifetime's amount of wisdom and knowledge. They will help today's readers navigate the present and the future, and they will do the same for the readers of the future, people who perhaps are not even alive yet as these words are written. What you bring to the reading is important, how you match Drucker's knowledge with your own.

The Age of Discontinuity: Guidelines to Our Changing Society (1969): This book has grown in influence in the years since it was published. It is about the broad changes Drucker identified that were happening in society at the end of the turbulent 1960s, as exemplified by the title to Chapter 1: "The End of Continuity." It represents Drucker's wide-ranging mind at its most free-flowing.

Drucker on Asia: A Dialogue between Peter Drucker and Isao Nakauchi (1997) contains fascinating material anticipating the future for Asia and the rest of the world. In particular, see Part 2, "Time to Reinvent."

The Drucker Lectures (2010): The final chapters are "The Future of the Corporation," Parts 1 to 4, from lectures given in 2003 at the Claremont Graduate University.

The Ecological Vision: Reflections on the American Condition (1993): This collection of essays and articles is mainly included here because of "The Unfashionable Kierkegaard" and the short, personal introduction that precedes it. In addition, see the superb five-chapter section "Japan as Society and Civilization," including "A View of Japan through Japanese Art."

Innovation and Entrepreneurship (1985): This classic book examines two related subjects that directly speak to creating the future, especially creating new value for organizations and society.

Landmarks of Tomorrow (1959) is a wide-ranging book about work, education, government, and society. Drucker returned to this theme a number of times, trying to make sense of where the world was heading, based on his interpretation of the available information. Nearly 30 years before *Innovation and Entrepreneurship,* Chapter 2 is "From Progress to Innovation." In the introduction for the 1996 edition of the book, he says, "In fact, my first title was *The Future That Has Already Happened,* and I dropped it only because it was too long to fit comfortably on a title page." The book cover on this edition proclaims it to be "A Report on the New 'Post-Modern' World."

Management Challenges for the 21st Century (1999): This is Drucker's last book of completely new material, and though in the introduction he claims it is not about the future, but rather the issues of tomorrow, a strong future-orientation is evident. In particular, there is Chapter 3 on "The Change Leader," with its concluding section, "Making the Future."

The revised edition of *Management* (2008) is an updated version of 1974's *Management: Tasks, Responsibilities, Practices.* It includes a somewhat shorter version of the chapter on the future in *Managing for Results.* Another chapter is "The Future of the Corporation and the Way Ahead," and the concluding chapter is "The Manager of Tomorrow."

Managing for Results (1964) contains one of Drucker's most prominent statements on the future: a chapter called "Making the Future Today." In it he explains the idea of "the future that has already happened" and also "making the future happen."

Managing for the Future: The 1990s and Beyond (1993): This was one of the periodic Drucker books that collected previously published articles, as well as interviews with him. The concluding chapter, in this case the afterword, is a reprint of a long briefing he wrote in 1990 for *The Economist*. (Its title is the same as the subtitle of the book.) In the preface, he writes that "every chapter in this book tries to create understanding of what changes are ahead and what they mean for the economy, people, markets, management, the organization. Every one of the chapters tries to create the understanding the executive needs to manage for tomorrow rather than for yesterday."

Managing in the Next Society (2002): This book, in structure, is similar to *Managing for the Future: The 1990s and Beyond* and *Managing in a Time of Great Change* in that it is a collection of previously published articles and interviews. It contains an important extended statement, "The Next Society," which was originally a guest feature in *The Economist*. (This piece also ran in another collection, 2003's *A Functioning Society: Selections from Sixty-Five Years of Writing on Community, Society, and Polity*.) The entire book is future-oriented and forward-thinking and includes a chapter based on a 1996 interview with *Inc.* magazine, "Entrepreneurs and Innovation."

Managing in a Time of Great Change (1995) has a similar format to *Managing for the Future: The 1990s and Beyond*. In particular, see Chapter 2, "Planning for Uncertainty," which originally appeared in the *Wall Street Journal*, and a wide-ranging interview about careers and more done with his longtime friend/associate T. George Harris, "The Post-Capitalist Executive."

Managing in Turbulent Times (1980): Although a somewhat-lesser-known work, this still has powerful material on the future, including the second chapter, "Managing for Tomorrow."

The New Realities (1989): Drucker explains in the preface that we were already into the next century in 1989 by virtue of changes in business, society, politics, government, education, and other areas. He writes: "This book does not focus on what to do tomorrow. It focuses on what to do *today* in contemplation of tomorrow. Within self-imposed limitations, it attempts to set the agenda."

Peter Drucker on the Profession of Management (1998): This collection from the *Harvard Business Review* includes the 1997 essay "The Future That Has Already Happened," as well as the interview "The Post-Capitalist Executive," also anthologized in *Managing in a Time of Great Change*.

Post-Capitalist Society (1993): Somewhat similar to *The New Realities* in its wide-ranging treatment of a variety of subjects, Drucker explains in the introduction that it is about a transformation taking place in many aspects of society. Two quotes from that introduction are particularly pertinent here: "It is not a history of the future. Rather, it is *a look at the present.*" Similarly, he ends the introduction with this: "Yet surely this is a time to *make the future*—precisely because everything is in flux. This is a time for action."

ONLINE RESOURCES

Here are the web addresses for selected sources that are mentioned in the book, especially in Chapter 2. They will all further your learning of and deepen your understanding about the future.

Awards, Honors, and Prizes

The Drucker Institute (Peter F. Drucker Award for Nonprofit Innovation)
http://www.druckerinstitute.com/what-we-do/nonprofit-innovation-award

The Economist (Innovation Awards)
http://www.economist.com/news/technology-quarterly/21567206-innovation-awards-our-annual-prizes-recognise-successful-innovators-eight

Encore.org (Purpose Prize)
http://www.encore.org/prize

Ernst & Young (Entrepreneur of the Year Award)
http://www.ey.com/US/en/About-us/Entrepreneurship/Entrepreneur-Of-The-Year

Financial Times/Goldman Sachs (Business Book of the Year)
http://www.goldmansachs.com/citizenship/business-book-award

The Frances Hesselbein Leadership Institute (Leader of the Future Award)
http://www.hesselbeininstitute.org/events/lotf/index.html

John Templeton Foundation (Templeton Prize)
http://www.templetonprize.org

MacArthur Foundation (Fellows Program, aka "Genius Grants")
http://www.macfound.org/programs/fellows

Nobel Foundation (Nobel Prizes)
http://www.nobelprize.org

Peter Drucker Society Europe (Drucker Challenge essay contest)
http://www.druckerchallenge.org

Skoll Foundation (Skoll Awards for Social Entrepreneurship)
http://www.skollfoundation.org/skoll-foundation-announces-2013-award-winners

TED (TEDPrize)
http://www.ted.com/prize

XPRIZE Foundation "Revolution through Competition"
http://www.xprize.org

Colleges and Universities

Forbes Top Colleges
http://www.forbes.com/top-colleges

Poets & Quants
http://poetsandquants.com

U.S. News & World Report Best Colleges A–Z
http://colleges.usnews.rankingsandreviews.com/best-colleges/sitemap?int=a557e6

Demographics and Statistics

American Fact Finder
http://factfinder2.census.gov/faces/nav/jsf/pages/index.xhtml

Bureau of Labor Statistics
http://www.bls.gov

Bureau of Labor Statistics; *TED: The Editor's Desk*
http://www.bls.gov/ted

International Monetary Fund
    http://www.imf.org/external/data.htm

Occupational Outlook Handbook
    http://www.bls.gov/ooh

O*Net
    http://www.onetonline.org

Statistical Abstract of the United States
    http://www.census.gov/compendia/statab
    http://cisupa.proquest.com/ws_display.asp?filter=Statistical%20
    Abstract

The Statistics Bureau and the Director-General for Policy Planning
    of Japan
    http://www.stat.go.jp/english

UK National Statistics Publication Hub
    http://www.statistics.gov.uk/hub/index.html

United Nations Demographic Yearbook
    http://unstats.un.org/unsd/demographic/products/dyb/dyb2.htm

U.S. government websites
    http://www.usa.gov
    http://www.data.gov

World Bank
    http://data.worldbank.org

Worldometers
    http://www.worldometers.info

Organizations and Think Tanks

A logical place to look for the future is on the websites of organizations, consultancies, special initiatives, and think tanks that make it their business to learn more about the future. This brief list is meant to show just some of the possibilities.

Accenture (Public Service for the Future)
   http://www.accenture.com/us-en/Pages/service-public-service-
   future.aspx

Burson-Marsteller (Future Perspective)
   http://burson-marsteller.eu/innovation-insights/future-
   perspective

Deloitte (Center for the Edge)
   http://www.deloitte.com/view/en_US/us/Insights/centers/centers-
   center-for-edge/index.htm

Foresight (future-oriented organization from the British government)
   http://www.bis.gov.uk/foresight

Future Leaders in Philanthropy
   http://www.networkflip.com

Future of Work (an initiative from Lynda Gratton, a professor at the
   London Business School)
   http://www.lyndagratton.com/research/research-2.html

The Future of Work (the research and advisory firm founded by
   former Harvard Business School professor Jim Ware)
   http://thefutureofwork.net

Futurethink
   http://futurethink.com

Insight Labs
   http://www.theinsightlabs.org

Institute for the Future
   http://www.iftf.org/home

McKinsey & Company (The Future of Work in Advanced
   Economies)
   http://www.mckinsey.com/insights/employment_and_growth/
   future_of_work_in_advanced_economies

Pew Research Center (especially useful for social trends, as well as a source of demographic data)
http://www.pewresearch.org

PSFK Labs (future-oriented consulting company)
http://labs.psfk.com

RAND Corporation
http://www.rand.org

World Future Society
http://www.wfs.org

Various Media-Related Sources

BBC Future
http://www.bbc.com/future

CNN What'sNext
http://whatsnext.blogs.cnn.com/

The Economist: The World in2013
http://www.economist.com/theworldin/2013

Fast Company Most Innovative Companies 2013
http://www.fastcompany.com/section/most-innovative-companies-2013

Forbes The World's Most Innovative Companies
http://www.forbes.com/special-features/innovative-companies.html

Miscellaneous

Appreciative Inquiry/David Cooperrider
http://www.davidcooperrider.com

Aurora WDC
http://aurorawdc.com

John Baldoni
   http://www.johnbaldoni.com

Herbert Benson/Benson-Henry Institute for Mind-Body Medicine
   http://www.massgeneral.org/bhi/about/benson.aspx

Jennifer Garvey Berger
   http://www.cultivatingleadership.co.nz/about-us/jennifer-
   garvey-berger

Jack Bergstrand/Brand Velocity
   http://brandvelocity.com/#/team/people/jack-bergstrand

Richard Branson
   http://www.virgin.com/richard-branson

Tom Butler-Bowdon
   http://nicholasbrealey.com/boston/Author/tom-butler-bowdon

Chase's Calendar of Events
   http://www.mhprofessional.com/templates/chases

Doug Conant
   http://conantleadership.com

Digimind
   http://www.digimind.com

The Drucker Institute
   http://www.druckerinstitute.com

The Drucker School
   http://www.cgu.edu/pages/130.asp

Drucker Workshop (Japan)
   http://drucker-ws.org

Frances Hesselbein Leadership Institute
   http://www.hesselbeininstitute.org

Howard Gardner
   http://howardgardner.com

Global Drucker Forum
    http://www.druckerforum.org
Sally Helgesen
    http://www.sallyhelgesen.com
The High Line
    http://www.thehighline.org
Jeremy Hunter
    http://jeremyhunter.net/about
Robert Kegan
    http://mindsatwork.com/index.php?page=about&family=us&c
    ategory=Who_Is_Minds_At_Work-reg-&display=14
Landmark College
    http://www.landmark.edu
Emi Makino
    http://www.cgu.edu/pages/6799.asp
Bruna Martinuzzi
    http://www.clarionenterprises.com/about-bruna.php
Mindful magazine
    http://www.mindful.org/mindful-magazine
Danielle Morrill
    http://www.daniellemorrill.com
Daniel Noll and Audrey Scott
    http://www.uncorneredmarket.com
Peter F. Drucker Academy (China)
    http://www.pfda.com.cn/english/aboutdrucker.html
Peter F. Drucker Society of Korea
    http://www.pdsociety.or.kr
Positive Psychology Center
    http://www.ppc.sas.upenn.edu

William Reed
   http://www.williamreed.jp/about

Search Inside Yourself Leadership Institute/Chade-Meng Tan
   http://www.siyli.org

Self-Efficacy/Albert Bandura
   http://www.uky.edu/#sleushe2/Pajares/self-efficacy.html

Huston Smith
   http://www.harpercollins.com/author/microsite/about.
   aspx?authorid=9210

Special Libraries Association /SLA Competitive Intelligence Division
   http://ci.sla.org

Jesse Lyn Stoner
   http://seapointcenter.com/jesse-lyn-stoner

Strategic and Competitive Intelligence Professionals/SCIP
   www.scip.org

The Roger K. Summit Scholarship
   http://proquest.com/en-US/aboutus/advocacy/summitscholar.
   shtml

Thinkers50
   http://www.thinkers50.com

Edward Tufte
   http://www.edwardtufte.com/tufte

Jean Watson/Watson Caring Science Institute and International Caring
   Consortium
   http://watsoncaringscience.org

The Thomas J. Watson Fellowship
   http://www.watsonfellowship.org/site/index.html

Jason Womack
   http://womackcompany.com

BIBLIOGRAPHY

Books by Peter F. Drucker

Drucker, Peter F. *Adventures of a Bystander*. New York: Harper & Row, 1979; revised ed., New York: John Wiley & Sons, 1998.

———. *The Age of Discontinuity: Guidelines to Our Changing Society*. New York: Harper & Row, 1969; revised ed., New Brunswick, NJ: Transaction Publishers, 1992.

———. *America's Next Twenty Years*. New York: Harper, 1957.

———. *The Ecological Vision: Reflections on the American Condition*. New Brunswick, NJ: Transaction Publishers, 1993.

———. *The Effective Executive*. New York: Harper & Row, 1967; rev. ed., New York: Collins, 2006.

———. *The Essential Drucker: the Best of Sixty Years of Peter Drucker's Essential Writings on Management*. New York: Harper Business, 2001.

———. *The Executive in Action*. New York: Harper Business, 1996.

———. *The Frontiers of Management: Where Tomorrow's Decisions Are Being Shaped Today*. New York: Truman Talley Books, 1986.

———. *A Functioning Society: Selections from Sixty-five Years of Writing on Community, Society, and Polity*. New Brunswick, NJ: Transaction Publishers, 2003.

———. *The Future of Industrial Man*. New York: The John Day Company, 1942; rev. ed., New Brunswick, NJ: Transaction Publishers, 1995.

———. *Innovation and Entrepreneurship: Practice and Principles*. New York: Harper & Row, 1985.

———. *Landmarks of Tomorrow: a Report on the New "Post-modern" World*. New York: Harper, 1959; rev. ed., New Brunswick, NJ: Transaction Publishers, 1996.

———. *The Last of All Possible Worlds: a Novel*. New York: Harper & Row, 1982.

———. *Management Challenges for the 21st Century*. New York: Harper Business, 1999.

———. *Management: Tasks, Responsibilities, Practices*. New York: Harper & Row, 1974.

———. *Managing for Results: Economic Tasks and Risk-Taking Decisions*. New York: Harper & Row, 1964.

———. *Managing for the Future: the 1990s and Beyond*. New York: Truman Talley Books/Dutton, 1993.

———. *Managing in a Time of Great Change*. New York: Truman Talley Books/Dutton, 1995.

———. *Managing in the Next Society*. New York: St. Martin's Press, 2002.

———. *Managing in Turbulent Times*. New York: Harper & Row, 1980.

———. *Managing the Non-Profit Organization: Principles and Practices*. New York: HarperCollins, 1990.

———. *Men, Ideas and Politics: Essays*. New York: Harper & Row, 1971.

———. *The New Realities: in Government and Politics, in Economics and Business, in Society and World View*. New York: Harper & Row, 1989.

———. *People and Performance: the Best of Peter Drucker on Management*. New York: Harper's College Press, 1977.

———. *Peter Drucker on the Profession of Management*. Boston: Harvard Business School Press, 1998.

———. *Post-Capitalist Society*. New York: Harper Business, 1993.

———. *The Practice of Management*. New York: Harper & Row, 1954.

———. *The Temptation to do Good*. New York: Harper & Row, 1984.

Drucker, Peter F., Jim Collins, Philip Kotler, et al. *The five most important questions you will ever ask about your organization*. New York: Leader to Leader Institute; San Francisco: Jossey-Bass, 2008.

Drucker, Peter F., and Joseph A. Maciariello. *The Daily Drucker: 366 Days of Insight and Motivation for Getting the Right Things Done.* New York: Harper Business, 2004.

——. *The Effective Executive in Action: a Journal for Getting the Right Things Done.* New York: Collins, 2006.

——. *Management.* rev. ed., New York: Collins, 2008.

Drucker, Peter F., and Isao Nakauchi. *Drucker on Asia: a Dialogue Between Peter Drucker and Isao Nakauchi.* Oxford, Newton, MA: Butterworth-Heinemann, 1997.

Drucker, Peter F., and Rick Wartzman. *The Drucker Lectures: Essential Lessons on Management, Society, and Economy.* New York: McGraw-Hill, 2010.

Books by Other Authors Mentioned in the Text

Allen, David. *Getting Things Done: the Art of Stress-Free Productivity.* New York: Viking, 2001.

Astin, Alexander W., Helen S. Astin, and Jennifer A. Lindholm. *Cultivating the Spirit: How College Can Enhance Students' Inner Lives.* San Francisco: Jossey-Bass, 2010.

Augustine of Hippo. *The Confessions of St. Augustine.* Trans. Rex Warner. New York: New American Library, 1963.

Baldoni, John. *Lead with Purpose: Giving Your Organization a Reason to Believe in Itself.* New York: American Management Association, 2012.

Barker, Joel Arthur. *Paradigms: The Business of Discovering the Future.* rev. ed., New York: Harper Business, 1993.

Bennis, Warren. *On Becoming a Leader.* Reading, MA: Addison-Wesley Pub. Co., 1989; rev. ed., Cambridge, MA: Perseus Pub, 2003.

Benson, Herbert. *The Relaxation Response.* New York: Morrow, 1975; rev. ed., with Miriam Z. Klipper. New York: Quill, 2001.

Bensoussan, Babette E., and Craig S. Fleisher. *Analysis Without Paralysis: 12 Tools to Make Better Strategic Decisions.* Upper Saddle River, NJ: FT Press, 2012.

Berger, Jennifer Garvey. *Changing on the Job: Developing Leaders for a Complex World*. Stanford, CA: Stanford Business Books, 2012.

Bergstrand, Jack. *Reinvent Your Enterprise Through Better Knowledge Work*. Atlanta: Brand Velocity 2010.

Blanchard, Ken, and Jesse Lyn Stoner. *Full Steam Ahead!: Unleash the Power of Vision in Your Work and in Your Life*. 2nd ed., San Francisco: Berrett-Koehler, 2011.

Branson, Richard. *Losing My Virginity: How I Survived, Had Fun, and Made a Fortune Doing Business My Way*. Updated ed., New York: Crown Business, 2011.

Bridges, William. *Transitions: Making Sense of Life's Changes*. 2nd ed., Cambridge, MA: Da Capo Press, 2004.

Buber, Martin. *I and Thou*. Trans. Walter Arnold Kaufmann. New York: Charles Scribner's Sons, 1970.

Buford, Bob. *Halftime: Changing Your Game Plan from Success to Significance*. Grand Rapids, Mich.: Zondervan, 1994; rev. ed., *Halftime: Moving from Success to Significance*. Grand Rapids, Mich.: Zondervan, 2008.

———. *Stuck in Halftime: Reinventing Your One and Only Life*. Grand Rapids, MI: Zondervan, 2001.

Burrus, Daniel, and John David Mann. *Flash Foresight: How to See the Invisible and Do the Impossible: Seven Radical Principles That Will Transform Your Business*. New York: Harper Business, 2011.

Butler-Bowdon, Tom. *50 Prosperity Classics: Attract It, Create It, Manage It, Share It*. London: Nicholas Brealey, 2010.

———. *50 Self-Help Classics: 50 Inspirational Books to Transform Your Life, From Timeless Sages to Contemporary Gurus*. London: Nicholas Brealey, 2003.

———. *50 Spiritual Classics: Timeless Wisdom from 50 Great Books of Inner Discovery, Enlightenment, and Purpose*. London: Nicholas Brealey, 2005.

———. *Never Too Late to be Great: the Power of Thinking Long*. London: Virgin Books, 2012.

Chase's Calendar of Events of 2014 with CD-ROM. New York: McGraw-Hill, 2013.

Christensen, Clayton M. *The Innovator's Dilemma: When New Technologies Cause Great Firms to Fail*. Boston: Harvard Business School Press, 1997.

Collins, Jim. *Good to Great: Why Some Companies Make the Leap—and Others Don't*. New York: Harper Business, 2001.

Conant, Douglas, and Mette Norgaard. *Touchpoints: Creating Powerful Leadership Connections in the Smallest of Moments*. San Francisco: Jossey-Bass, 2011.

Csikszentmihalyi, Mihaly. *Creativity: Flow and the Psychology of Discovery and Invention*. New York: HarperCollins, 1996.

———. *Flow: the Psychology of Optimal Experience*. New York: Harper & Row, 1990.

David, Joshua, and Robert Hammond. *High Line: the Inside Story of New York City's Park in the Sky*. New York: Farrar, Straus & Giroux, 2011.

De Pree, Max. *Leadership is an Art*. New York: Doubleday, 1989; rev. ed., New York: Crown Business, 2004.

Dweck, Carol S. *Mindset: the New Psychology of Success*. New York: Random House, 2006.

Franklin, Daniel, and John Andrews. *Megachange: the World in 2050*. Hoboken, NJ: Wiley, 2012.

Freedman, Marc. *The Big Shift: Navigating the New Stage Beyond Midlife*. New York: PublicAffairs, 2011.

———. *Encore: Finding Work That Matters in the Second Half of Life*. New York: Public Affairs, 2007.

Gardner, Dan. *Future Babble: Why Expert Predictions are Next to Worthless, and You Can do Better*. New York: Dutton, 2011.

Gardner, Howard. *Creating Minds: an Anatomy of Creativity Seen through the Lives of Freud, Einstein, Picasso, Stravinsky, Eliot, Graham, and Gandhi.* New York: Basic Books, 1993; rev. ed., New York: Basic Books, 2011.

Gardner, Howard. *Five Minds for the Future.* Boston: Harvard Business School Press, 2007.

Gardner, Howard, and Emma Laskin. *Leading Minds: an Anatomy of Leadership.* New York: Basic Books, 1995; rev. ed., New York: Basic Books, 2011.

Grudin, Robert. *Time and the Art of Living.* Cambridge, MA: Harper & Row, 1982.

Hamel, Gary, and C. K. Prahalad. *Competing for the Future.* Boston: Harvard Business School Press, 1994.

Helgesen, Sally. *The Female Advantage: Women's Ways of Leadership.* New York: Doubleday Currency, 1990.

———. *The Web of Inclusion.* New York: Currency/Doubleday, 1995.

Hesselbein, Frances, Marshall Goldsmith, Richard Beckhard, et al., ed. *The Community of the Future.* San Francisco: Jossey-Bass, 1998.

Hesselbein, Frances, *Hesselbein on Leadership.* San Francisco: Jossey-Bass, 2002.

———. *More Hesselbein on Leadership.* San Francisco: Jossey-Bass, 2012.

———. *My Life in Leadership: the Journey and Lessons Learned Along the Way.* San Francisco: Jossey-Bass, 2011.

Hesselbein, Frances, and Marshall Goldsmith, eds. *The Leader of the Future 2: Visions, Strategies, and Practices for the New Era.* San Francisco: Jossey-Bass, 2006.

Hesselbein, Frances, Marshall Goldsmith, and Iain Somerville, eds. *Leading for Innovation and Organizing for Results.* San Francisco: Jossey-Bass, 2002.

Iwasaki, Natsumi. *What if a Female Manager of a High School Baseball Team Read Drucker's "Management."* Tokyo: Diamond, 2009.

Johansen, Bob. *Leaders Make the Future: Ten New Leadership Skills for an Uncertain World*. San Francisco: Berrett-Koehler Publishers, 2012.

Jung, C. G., and Aniela Jaffé. *Memories, Dreams, Reflections*. New York: Vintage Books, 1989.

Kegan, Robert, and Lisa Laskow Lahey. *Immunity to Change: How to Overcome It and Unlock Potential in Yourself and Your Organization*. Boston: Harvard Business Press, 2009.

Kierkegaard, Søren. *Training in Christianity: and the Edifying Discourse which "Accompanied" It*. Trans. Walter Lowrie. Princeton, NJ: Princeton University Press, 1944.

Kouzes, James M., and Barry Z. Posner. *The Truth About Leadership: the No-Fads, Heart-of-the-Matter Facts You Need to Know*. San Francisco: Jossey-Bass, 2010.

Kurzweil, Ray. 2012. *How to Create a Mind: the Secret of Human Thought Revealed*. New York: Viking.

Maciariello, Joseph A. *Work and Human Nature: Leadership and Management Practices at ServiceMaster and the Drucker Tradition*. Pasadena, CA: De Pree Leadership Center, 2002.

Maciariello, Joseph A., and Karen E. Linkletter. *Drucker's Lost Art of Management: Peter Drucker's Timeless Vision For Building Effective Organizations*. New York: McGraw-Hill, 2011.

Martinuzzi, Bruna. *The Leader as a Mensch: Become the Kind of Person Others Want to Follow*. San Francisco: Six Seconds Emotional Intelligence Press, 2009.

———. *Presenting with Credibility: Practical Tools and Techniques For Effective Presentations*. San Francisco: Six Seconds Emotional Intelligence Press, 2012.

Maurer, Robert. *One Small Step Can Change Your Life: the Kaizen Way*. New York: Workman, 2004.

Maurer, Robert, and Leigh Ann Hirschman. *The Spirit of Kaizen: Creating Lasting Excellence One Small Step at a Time*. New York: McGraw-Hill, 2013.

McGonigal, Jane. *Reality is Broken: Why Games Make Us Better and How They Can Change the World*. New York: Penguin Press, 2011.

Pearce, Craig L., Joseph A. Maciariello, and Hideki Yamawaki, eds. *The Drucker Difference: What the World's Greatest Management Thinker Means to Today's Business Leaders*. New York: McGraw-Hill, 2010.

Pollard, C. William. *The Soul of the Firm*. New York: Harper Business, 1996.

ProQuest Statistical Abstract of the United States. Lanham, MD: Bernan Press, 2013.

Rosenstein, Bruce. *Living in More Than One World: How Peter Drucker's Wisdom Can Inspire and Transform Your Life*. San Francisco: Berrett-Koehler, 2009.

Schwartz, Peter. *The Art of the Long View*. New York: Doubleday/ Currency, 1991.

Seligman, Martin E. P. *Authentic Happiness: Using the New Positive Psychology to Realize Your Potential For Lasting Fulfillment*. New York: Free Press, 2002.

———. *Flourish: a Visionary New Understanding of Happiness and Well-being*. New York: Free Press, 2011.

———. *Learned Optimism: How to Change Your Mind and your Life*. New York: Knopf, 1991.

Sims, Peter. *Little Bets: How Breakthrough Ideas Emerge From Small Discoveries*. New York: Free Press, 2011.

Smith, Huston, and Jeffery Paine. *Tales of Wonder: Adventures Chasing the Divine: an Autobiography*. New York: HarperOne, 2009.

Smith, Huston. *Why Religion Matters: the Fate of the Human Spirit in an Age of Disbelief*. New York: HarperCollins, 2001.

———. *The Religions of Man*. New York: Harper, 1958.

———. *The World's Religions*. 50th anniversary ed., New York: HarperCollins, 2009.

Sommers, Cecily. *Think Like a Futurist: Know What Changes, What Doesn't, and What's Next.* San Francisco: Jossey-Bass, 2012.

Suzuki, Shunryu, and Trudy Dixon. *Zen Mind, Beginner's Mind.* New York, Walker/Weatherhill, 1970; rev. ed., Boston: Shambhala, 2010.

Taleb, Nassim Nicholas. *The Black Swan: the Impact of the Highly Improbable.* New York: Random House, 2010.

Tan, Chade-Meng. *Search Inside Yourself: the Unexpected Path to Achieving Success, Happiness (and World Peace).* New York: HarperOne, 2012.

Tapscott, Don, and Anthony D. Williams. *Wikinomics: How Mass Collaboration Changes Everything.* New York: Portfolio, 2006.

Toffler, Alvin. *Future Shock.* New York: Random House, 1970.

Tolle, Eckhart. *The Power of Now: a Guide to Spiritual Enlightenment.* Novato, CA: New World Library, 1999.

Tufte, Edward R. *The Cognitive Style of PowerPoint: Pitching Out Corrupts Within,* 2nd Ed., Cheshire, CT: Graphics Press, 2006.

———. *The Visual Display of Quantitative Information.* Cheshire, CT: Graphics Press, 2001.

U.S. Department of Labor, Bureau of Labor Statistics. *Occupational Outlook Handbook* 2013–2014 Washington, DC, New York: McGraw-Hill, 2013.

Warren, Rick. *The Purpose-Driven Life: What on Earth Am I Here For?* Grand Rapids, MI: Zondervan, 2002.

Wartzman, Rick. *Drucker: a Life in Pictures.* New York: McGraw-Hill, 2013.

Womack, Jason W. *Your Best Just Got Better: Work Smarter, Think Bigger, Make More.* Hoboken, NJ: Wiley, 2012.

Zaleski, Philip. *The Best Spiritual Writing 2013.* New York: Penguin Books, 2013.

Articles and Websites

Anderson, Chris. "The Man who Makes the Future: Wired Icon Marc Andreessen," *Wired.* May 2012. http://www.wired.com/business/2012/04/ff_andreessen/ (accessed July 31, 2013).

Baldoni, John. "Steel Your Purpose," *Leader to Leader.* 2012 (Spring): 33–37.

Bandura, Albert. "Commentary: On the Psychosocial Impact and Mechanisms of Spiritual Modeling," *International Journal for the Psychology of Religion* 13 (2003): 167–173.

———. "Social Cognitive Theory in Cultural Context," *Applied Psychology* 51(2002): 269–290.

"Cap and Gown Day on Campus: 410 Given Degrees at U of S; Graduates Termed "True Capitalists" by Professor at NYU," *The Scranton Times.* 1 June 1964, Sec. 1, pg. 3, 10.

Conant, Doug, and Mette Norgaard. "TouchPoints: The Power of Leading in the Moment," *Leader to Leader.* 2012 (Winter): 44–49.

Drucker, Peter. "The Delusion of Profits," *Wall Street Journal,* 5 February, 1975, pg. 10.

———. "The Future That Has Already Happened," *The Futurist.* 32 (8) (1998): 16–18.

———. "The Future That Has Already Happened," *Harvard Business Review.* 75 (1997): 20, 22, 24.

———. "How to be an Employee," *Fortune.* May (1952): 126–127.

———. "Memo to Managers: Find Outside Pleasure," *New York Times.* 5 May, 1974, sec. E, p. 21.

———. "The New Society of Organizations," *Harvard Business Review.* 70 (1992): 95–104.

———. "The Next Society," *The Economist.* November 1, 2001. http://www.economist.com/node/770819 (accessed July 31, 2013).

——. "Planning for Uncertainty," *Wall Street Journal.* 22 July, 1992, Se. A, pg. 14.

——. "The Post-Capitalist Executive," [Interview by T. George Harris] *Harvard Business Review.* 71 (1993) (3): 114–22.

——. "The Romantic Generation," *Harper's.* (May) 232 (1966): 12–23.

——. "The Unfashionable Kierkegaard," *Sewanee Review.* 57 (1949): 587–602.

——. "What Business Can Learn from Nonprofits," *Harvard Business Review.* 67 (1989): 88–93.

——. "What Makes an Effective Executive?," *Harvard Business Review.* 82 (2004): 58–63.

Drucker, Peter F., Esther Dyson, Charles Handy, Paul Saffo, and Peter M. Senge. "Looking ahead: Implications of the Present," *Harvard Business Review.* 75 (1997): 18.18–32.

Fernandez, Susana. "Peter Drucker's Leap *to* Faith: Examining the Origin of His Purpose-Driven Life and its Impact on his Views of Management," *Journal of Management History.* 15 (2009): 404–419.

Garvey Berger, Jennifer. "Cultivating Wisdom," *Leader to Leader.* 2012 (Fall): 40–44.

Gendron, George. "Flashes of Genius." *Inc.,* May 15, 1996. http://www.inc.com/magazine/19960515/2083.html (accessed July 31, 2013).

Goetz, Thomas. "How to Spot the Future," *Wired.* May 2012. http://www.wired.com/business/2012/04/ff_spotfuture/(accessed July 31, 2013).

Hunter, Jeremy. "It Can Transform Your Relationship With Yourself, With Other People, and With the Pressures of the Modern World, But … Is Mindfulness Good for Business?," *Mindful.* 1 (April): 2013: 52–59.

Helgesen, Sally. "Leading in 24/7: What is Required?," *Leader to Leader*. 2012 (Summer): 38–43.

"The Importance of Happiness in the Workplace," *Leader to Leader*. 2012 (Winter): 62–63.

Krugman, Paul. "Age of Anxiety," *New York Times*, 28 November, 2005, p. 19.

Lenzner, Robert, and Stephen S. Johnson. "Peter Drucker—Still the Youngest of Minds—With The Economy on a Roll, the Old Master Has Some Sobering Visions: The Rich Better Listen Up," *Forbes*. 159 (1997): 122.

Meynhardt, Timo. "The Practical Wisdom of Peter Drucker: Roots in the Christian Tradition," *Journal of Management Development* 29 (2010): 616–625.

Oman, Doug, and Carl E. Thoresen. "Spiritual Modeling: A Key to Spiritual and Religious Growth?," [invited essay] *International Journal for the Psychology of Religion*. 13 (2003): 149–165.

Porath, Christine, Gretchen Spreitzer, Cristina Gibson, and Flannery G. Garnett. "Thriving at Work: Toward its Measurement, Construct Validation, and Theoretical Refinement," *Journal of Organizational Behavior*. 33 (2012): 250–275.

Romar, Edward. "Managerial Harmony: the Confucian Ethics of Peter F. Drucker," *Journal of Business Ethics*. 51 (2004): 199–210.

Rosenstein, Bruce. "Drucker's Reinventing Himself at Age 95," *USA Today*, 15 November, 2004, sec. B, p. 06.

Salim, Amanda. "Quem será o próximo Peter Drucker?," *Revista Administradores*, year 1, (April 2011): 32–37. http://www.administradores.com.br/noticias/administracao-e-negocios/quem-sera-o-proximo-peter-drucker/58229/(accessed August 19, 2013)

Stern, Stefan. "Lunch with the FT: Lynda Gratton," *Financial Times*, 5 February, 2010 pg. 3.

Womack, Jason W. "Your Best Just Got Better," *Leader to Leader*. 2013 (Winter): 43–48.

Blogs and Special Issues

Bennis, Warren. 2013. "Does religion belong in the B-school curriculum?"

BloombergBusinessweek (blog), January 13, 2013. http://www.businessweek.com/articles/2013-01-22/does-religion-belong-in-the-b-school-curriculum (accessed July 31, 2013).

BRAIN initiative. 2013. http://www.whitehouse.gov/infographics/brain-initiative (accessed July 31, 2013).

Brussat, Frederic, and Mary Ann Brussat. 2013. The Best Spiritual Books of 2012. *Spirituality & Practice.* http://www.spiritualityandpractice.com/books/features.php?id=23617 (accessed July 31, 2013).

Fortune. 2013. Future issue. January 14, 2013. http://money.cnn.com/magazines/fortune/fortune_archive/2013/01/14/toc.html (accessed July 31, 2013).

The Futurist. 2013. 2020 Visionaries. http://www.wfs.org/Dec09-Jan10/Vision1.htm (accessed July 31, 2013).

Landmark College. 2013. Office of the president. http://www.landmark.edu/why-landmark/leadership/office-of-the-president/ (accessed July 31, 2013).

Morrill, Danielle. "I Don't Do That Job Anymore." *Danielle Morrill* (blog) http://www.daniellemorrill.com/2013/02/i-dont-do-that-job-anymore (Accessed August 22, 2013).

National Center on the Universal Design for Learning. 2013. What is UDL? http://www.udlcenter.org/aboutudl/whatisudl (accessed July 31, 2013).

PBS. 2011. Bill Moyers: *The Wisdom of Faith with Huston Smith.* http://www.shoppbs.org/product/index.jsp?productId=12003071 (accessed July 31, 2013).

Positive Psychology Center. 2013. Frequently asked questions. http://www.ppc.sas.upenn.edu/faqs.htm (accessed July 31, 2013).

Reed, William. 2010. Idea Marathon (blog). *Creative Career Path,* September 15, 2010. http://www.daijob.com/en/columns/williamreed/article/2485 (accessed July 31, 2013).

Reynolds, Garr. 2013. *Presentation Zen* blog. http://www.presentationzen.com/about.html (accessed July 31, 2013).

Spirituality in Higher Education. 2013. A national study of spirituality in higher education: students' search for meaning and purpose. http://spirituality.ucla.edu/findings/ (accessed July 31, 2013).

USA Today. 2012. Special section. USA Tomorrow, September 15, 2012. http://www.usatoday.com/topic/6F6D6196-C085-40F6-A391-0-AAA08F20E11/usa-tomorrow/ (accessed July 31, 2013).

Watson, Jean. 2007. Watson's "Ten Caritas™ Processes." http://watson-caringscience.org/about-us/caring-science-definitions-processes-theory/ (accessed July 31, 2013).

INDEX

Willow Creek Community Church, 133

Window metaphor, 102–104, 106

Wolfram Alpha, 55

Wolfram, Stephen, 55

Womack, Jason, 81–83

Work and workplace

activities outside work and, 41, 152

creating future beyond, 127–128

holistic look beyond, 151–153

investigative work, 114

producing impressive body of work, 44

thriving at work, 74–75

transformation tools for working smarter, 80–86

work-life integration, 20–21

Workaholic, 33

World Bank, 44

World Health Partners, 107

The World in..., 53

World War II, 23

The World's Religions (Smith), 138, 139

Zaleski, Philip, 136

Zen, 22–23, 30, 87

Zuckerberg, Mark, 108